AGAINST THE FLOW

AGAINST THE FLOW

A New Strategic Framework for
Business Success in the 21st Century

YUDA TUVAL

ORION
BUSINESS
BOOKS

First published in Great Britain in 1999 by
Orion Business
An imprint of The Orion Publishing Group Ltd
Orion House, 5 Upper St Martin's Lane, London WC2H 9EA

A CIP catalogue record for this book is available
from the British Library.

ISBN 0-75282-071-0

Typeset at The Spartan Press Ltd, Lymington, Hants
Printed and bound in Great Britain by
Creative Print and Design (Wales), Ebbw Vale

CONTENTS

Acknowledgements   vii

Preface   ix

PART ONE: A NEW BUSINESS FRAMEWORK

Introduction   3

1   Why the mainstream is bad for you   13

2   Defying the current   33

3   What's stopping you?   59

4   A new kind of competition   93

5   Reworking relationships   127

6   What next?   151

Interlude: The Fresh Horizons story   171

PART TWO: PRACTICAL GUIDANCE

7   Managing people against the flow   183

8   Financial control against the flow   193

9   Using information technology against the flow   201

Index   211

ACKNOWLEDGEMENTS

There are many people to whom I owe a great deal for the help they gave me in this work.

First, I would like to express my deepest thanks to Rupert Morris and the staff at Clarity for ensuring that ideas are expressed simply as well as removing jargon which gets in the way of the reader's understanding. Rupert also persuaded two publishing firms to compete for the right to publish. Despite my frequent absences and the constant pressure of other work, he guided the entire project from concept to publication in a mere 18 months.

Secondly, I owe a great deal to my colleagues and staff at KPMG, who have offered valuable ideas and practical help. Particularly noteworthy were the contributions of Ketan Patel, Jean-Herve Jenn, Angie Cadiz, Nick Griffin, Anna Coen, Robert Fedder and Nada Spendal.

Special thanks go to Fiona Clarke for managing the entire logistics element of this work in very difficult circumstances.

I would also like to thank Eddie Oliver and Mike Rake for their sponsorship and moral encouragement.

Last but not least, I would like to thank Martin Liu from Orion Publishing for his critiques of the book and for encouraging me to dare where I would have been more prudent.

Needless to say, the ideas expressed in this book are mine and in no way commit the individuals who have helped me, nor KPMG.

PREFACE

Yuda Tuval is one of the most stimulating people I have met in all my years in business. He loves good food, good wine and a good argument! He has an outstanding intellect and is engaged in a never-ending journey of understanding. Knowing what happened in practice is never enough for Yuda; he can't rest until he knows why it happened in theory. He is right in this. One has to be clear about why something happened – how the rational, emotional and political forces interacted in the particular circumstances. Then you can build a generic model and then you can tell whether the results are replicable.

Yuda goes where his reasoning takes him. He does not accept others' conclusions; he is not swayed by conventional wisdom. The conclusions he draws are not always comfortable. You, his reader, will not agree with everything he says any more than I do. But you will find his thought processes invigorating and his conclusions challenging.

In this book, Yuda urges you to swim against the flow. He argues that the business world is made up of shapers, adapters and victims. We can't all be shapers. As Yuda says, without followers there would be no leaders. But we must all try to avoid being victims. This book will help you understand the dangers that lie in wait for the herd and choose the ground on which you want to compete. It looks at the tools business leaders have available to them to guide their companies towards their chosen futures.

A word of warning. Yuda tells of the limitations of some popular management tools, processes and systems: market research, benchmarking, enterprise resource systems etc. But please note that he does not argue against the use of such processes; he argues against their unthinking use. Focus on the business issue – on the result you want to secure. Then find the right tool for that particular job.

I admire the clarity with which Yuda expresses his views. He is able to explain complex, sophisticated concepts in simple, straightforward language. This is something we at KPMG value very highly. We have no time for people who dress up their conclusions in obscure, jargon-laden language. I don't believe businessmen or women are impressed by this. On the contrary, I think the communicator has the responsibility to get the message across. KPMG says that it's time for clarity. This book is a good example of what we mean.

When you have read this book you will know how to swim against the flow. And you will also know Yuda Tuval. As Pascal said, 'Quand on voit le style naturel, on est tout étonné et ravi, car on s'attendait de voir un auteur, et on trouve un homme' – When we see a natural style, we are quite surprised and delighted for we expected to see an author and we find a man.

Colin Sharman
KPMG International Chairman
May 1999

PART ONE

A New Business Framework

INTRODUCTION

What is this book about? It is an invitation to you, the chief executive or aspiring chief executive, to dare to go against the flow. But it is a loaded invitation – for the alternative, we believe, is failure.

For many executives, the business world changes at such an alarming rate that it can seem like a full-time job just to keep up; the competition grows ever more intense and it becomes harder and harder to maintain an edge. The winning formula we all seek seems to be just out of reach, and, at the very moment that you think you may be glimpsing it, the vision recedes as you are obliged once more to wrestle with the day-to-day cares of running a business. Without help, you sense you might be pulled into the clinging bog of crisis management. You know that that way lies a slow and agonising death, and yet you feel powerless to resist. This book can help you – but only if you are willing to use your imagination.

There is no sure-fire formula for success. Many of the most enterprising and successful businesses have failed at the first attempt. And who knows which of today's outstanding success stories will be brought crashing down in the near future? Everyone in business accepts a modicum of risk, and that means operating to some extent on the basis of trial and error. But there *is* a sure-fire formula for failure: risk nothing, try to keep up with your competitors, and go with the flow. Nemesis may take its time to arrive, but your victim status is assured.

In the closing decades of the twentieth century, business leaders have struggled to adapt to rapidly changing circumstances and dramatic new possibilities opened up by new technology. They have downsized, restructured, re-engineered, merged and demerged – almost invariably following the prevailing business current. Yet still they search for the Holy Grail, the framework that will enable them to compete successfully over the long term. And, as long as they continue to follow the mainstream, they will search in vain.

Our premise is that the mainstream of business can lead you in all sorts of directions, some desirable, some undesirable. But because you have no control of the flow you have no way of ensuring that you will be able to travel in your chosen direction.

Consider your industry or market sector as a stream. That stream will change shape and run at different speeds as it journeys through rapids and over waterfalls or meanders through meadows. It may suddenly take quite a different direction when a discontinuity is created – as when state industries are privatised, or airlines start offering financial services. It may grow and widen into a mighty river. It may swiftly become absorbed into a bigger stream, river or lake. It may run into a bog or marsh and die out. Or it may become polluted or clogged with weeds. If we simply surrender to the pull of the current, we may be pulled the wrong way – over the rapids, or into the bog. Our survival, like that of the trout or salmon, depends on our ability to swim upstream, against the flow, until we find an environment conducive to our development.

What does this mean in business terms? It means, to begin with, that you must be prepared to break with some basic, almost sacred, assumptions – assumptions that lie behind almost all classical business strategy.

The first of these is that there is a future – a business world that will be shaped by forces largely beyond our control. Our aim, it is assumed, is to study existing trends and make the best guess we can as to how that future might develop. Then we might have a chance of adapting to those changes better than our competitors.

Can't argue with that, can we? Actually, we certainly can. For although it sounds plausible enough we believe that our survival demands an entirely different approach.

We believe there are as many futures as your imagination will allow. They fall, almost invariably, into one of three categories. The first category is more of the same – the same game, played according to the same rules – and if you opt for these futures you will in due course become a victim. Then there is a second category, in which you manage, to some extent, to change the rules of the game; by being a skilful adapter, you can influence these futures, and prosper in the process. Finally, by changing the game itself, by creating a discontinuity so that you are out on your own, playing a new game according to new rules, you can be a shaper, capable of turning your vision into reality.

Success at the dawn of the twenty-first century is about an attitude of mind. Consider the diagram overleaf. In one corner you will find the victims, inhabiting an illusory zone of comfort, playing the same game as everyone else, according to the same rules. They prefer the least risky options, emotionally, politically and probably technically, too. These are people who lack the imagination to challenge received wisdom. They may be doing the same things they have been doing successfully for many years, or they may be aping others. They may appear to be competent, model professionals – but their time is running out. The stream, you will notice, runs towards them. This is where you will end up if you do not go against the flow.

Moving upstream to the next box – the one marked 'adapter' – is the first significant step to survival. If you can challenge the received wisdom to the point of getting the rules changed, you are acquiring a measure of control over your own destiny. Having worked to get the

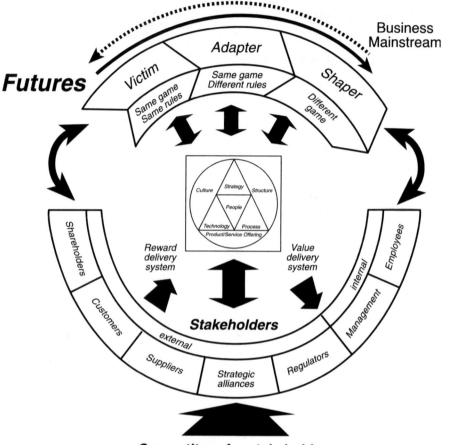

A new business framework

rules changed, you become one of the few who know them – if not the only one. As a result you should be considerably better placed than most of your rivals.

The shapers – that elite band who have managed not only to change the rules but to change the game itself – lie further upstream. Having created a discontinuity, they are uniquely placed to exploit it. To be a shaper is a noble aim, but it is not the only way to succeed. What matters above all is that you go against the flow, leaving the victims behind you, towards the space occupied by the shapers. It is, as I have said, all about your attitude of mind. You must begin by asking the right questions – not the everyday ones that anchor you in the very reality from which you need to escape. Why are you here? You need a sense of purpose and identity beyond the fact that, say, you are a bank, a motor manufacturer or a management consultancy. Above all, you must try to define your relationship with your customers. What is it that you offer them? What do they get from you that they can't get from any other source? What value do you uniquely provide? And, if you don't provide any unique value, why not? If your products or services can be readily imitated, you will become a mere commodity producer, liable to be squeezed on price by your competition. We explore these matters in Chapters 1 and 2, as we help you to choose your future, not least by taking control of the customer relationship.

Having chosen the future you want, what should you do next? The short answer is: bring it to the present faster than your competitors can react. The longer answer, detailed in Chapter 3, is to use your organisation's available levers of change to bring about your chosen future as quickly as is organisationally feasible. Taking too long over change can be even more damaging than making no change at all. This is where a lack of imagination can be fatal, and this is where many businesses fail. Why? Because you will never retain control of your customer relationship unless all your internal forces are aligned in pursuit of your corporate goals. The seven levers of change are the various components of your business that can either help or impede your progress. Neglect just one of these, and your organisation can be paralysed. Pay them due attention and you and your staff will be empowered, ready to go against the flow.

Assuming that you have passed through these two stages, the third and final stage concerns competition. It begins with the question: who are we doing this for, anyway? Traditionally, we compete for customers, in the belief that 'the customer knows best'. Using market research, we ask them what they want, then try to produce the right mix of products and services to satisfy them, adjusting price to allow for the maximum profit consistent with market acceptance. There are two crucial assumptions here: first that competition is one-dimensional in that we are all aiming at the same target – customers; secondly, that to find out what they want all we have to do is to ask them. In Chapters 4 and 5, we challenge both these assumptions in order to enable you to choose and implement your desired future.

Competition, we believe, is multidimensional. Organisations have a number of different stakeholders – not only customers, but also shareholders, suppliers, employees, business managers, regulators and strategic allies. We have to compete for all these different stakeholders at the same time, developing different value propositions for each one. Not only do these stakeholders require different value propositions, and, therefore, different value-delivery systems but, to make life even more difficult, their requirements tend to be in conflict more often than not. To take an obvious example, if you increase the pay of your employees, you will find it more difficult to offer your customers price cuts. We have to face the fact that we cannot maximise value to each stakeholder; instead, we must optimise the entire portfolio the best we can. One more complication is that we are competing with many different kinds of organisation.

We also challenge the notion of classical marketing, based on the idea of asking the customer. Most customers have an idea of their needs and wants that is bounded by their own experience; hardly ever do they imagine products or services that do not yet exist. If, for a moment, they think 'Wouldn't it be neat if . . . ?' they rapidly dismiss such notions, filing them under the heading of wishful thinking. No customer, for instance, ever suggested to Sony that they should develop the Walkman; nor did any customer demand that Airbus introduce fly-by-wire technology. Moreover, customers tend to limit their demands to what they expect from you: no one ever asked General Electric, Virgin or Marks & Spencer to sell them financial products. Asking the customer, therefore, may be necessary but it is certainly not sufficient.

In this book we investigate new and different approaches – sometimes involving the redefinition of business relationships – to help identify our stakeholders' real needs without actually asking them. These new approaches enable us to define the new value propositions we need in order to create the future we want.

Such, then, is the three-part framework that can be your survival guide. It involves choosing your future, priming your levers of change, and delivering stakeholder value propositions. That is the order in which we shall discuss the three parts in this book. But business life is not linear. With a business start-up, you might have the opportunity to set out as a shaper, align your levers of change, and deliver your value propositions to stakeholders. But this is unusual. Mature businesses cannot go back to square one every time they embark on radical change, but this does not mean they cannot go against the flow. Hence the diagram on page 6, represented as a cycle. This recognises that you can enter our framework at any stage of the business cycle. For instance, it may be in redefining your relationships with your suppliers that you begin to go against the flow. Or it may be in developing new value propositions for your staff that you realign your business, and recognise new strategic possibilities. This, therefore, is the master diagram to which we shall return throughout Part One.

In Part Two, we shall take a closer look at the three key operational areas, of people, finance and technology. Each of these subjects is well worthy of a book in itself, but we do not intend any such in-depth investigation. Instead, we have simply selected a few practical issues we believe business leaders ignore at their peril.

CHAPTER 1 – DIGEST

Why the mainstream is bad for you

Key message:

In the new business world, going with the flow of established business thought is the sure route to extinction. When exploiting discontinuities is the key to success, you need to be able to go against the flow.

Why?

Because the changing nature of change has made it impossible to survive by playing the game by the same old rules. If you can't change the game, at least try to make your own rules.

What?

- Business's fashion victims – fads and forces
- The attractions of backwaters
- Invisible competitors
- Understanding and creating discontinuities
- The illusion of control
- How some of the mighty fell

So what?

So don't be a victim. Don't be distracted by fads or swept along by the prevailing business currents. Work towards your own vision of the future.

CHAPTER 1

Why the mainstream is bad for you

The changing nature of change

'Adapt or die' is the popular slogan. Its original author was H. G. Wells, who actually wrote: 'Adapt or perish, now as ever, is Nature's inexorable imperative.' That was in 1946, and, where Nature is concerned, it retains the ring of truth. In business, however, where the natural world has long since been left behind, Wells's adage no longer tells the full story. In the twenty-first century, businesses will need to do more than adapt in order to stay alive. Suddenly, the old maxims, tried and trusted business methods, classical strategies – yes, even what passes for wisdom in the top business schools – are as much use as an umbrella in a hurricane. This is because of the changing nature of change.

Since midway through the twentieth century, we have learned that nothing in business really stands still, and that change is the norm. Previously, the fact that technology, transport and communication all took time to take effect had created an illusion of stability. As these things speeded up, we saw the illusion for what it was, and we began to grasp the notion of continuous change.

New questions arose. How could we identify change? How could we analyse it? How could we control it? How could we implement it? And how could we manage it? Change management became one of the pillars of the consultancy revolution of the 1980s and 1990s. It remains a key competency within many leading firms of consultants, and understandably so, with the ever-present need to reconcile the rational, political, social, emotional and personal elements involved in any substantial change project.

The pace of change has become our overriding concern. More vital questions have sprung up: How much change can we deal with at any one time? How quickly can we adapt? What is the innate capacity of our organisation to deal with change?

Takeover fever

This obsession with change has had various unfortunate consequences. The mid-to-late 1980s saw the first serious outbreak of takeover fever, which took hold again in the late 1990s. Both were periods of bull stock markets when it was easy for firms to engineer all-paper transactions. In the frenzied atmosphere, people felt the only way to stay ahead of the market was to change size – to grow, in other words – and the easiest way to grow was to acquire. It worked as long as the market kept rising, and, if it crashed, everyone would crash together, so no one would have an advantage. With the economies of the world becoming more and more global, there was a need to rationalise, to avoid fragmentation, and achieve economies of scale wherever possible. Investment bankers and others keen to make money out of these transactions found it easy enough to come up with all kinds of paper synergies. But many of these synergies proved as illusory as the stable market conditions that traditional businesses had relied upon decades earlier.

There were two main types of takeover. The activities of the Hanson

Group in the late 1980s were typical of the first type – the shareholder-led takeover that relied on diversification. The Hanson Group did a fantastic job for its shareholders, picking winners, spreading risk and doing all the things a shrewd investor might desire. Many shareholders in the Hanson Group made lots of money, but few of its companies made any lasting improvements. Certainly none made quantum leaps or significant and lasting changes in their industries. The remarkable success of corporate raiders like James Hanson and James Goldsmith helped to create the pervasive cult of shareholder value – which is in itself a reasonable aspiration, but by no means the Holy Grail of business. Far more important for most executives to concentrate on those areas where value can be added to a business.

The difference is clear enough. Whereas many investors would pick the renowned stock-market wizard Warren Buffett to manage their portfolios, chief executives would not immediately turn to the same man to manage their companies. It would be like appointing the racing tipster to run the newspaper.

The second main type of takeover was on grounds of size – responding to the notion that businesses need a certain scale, a certain presence, in order to compete in an increasingly global market. Clearly, there have been industries in which small operators have found themselves squeezed by the big boys: the motor industry, for instance, where the announcement of a merger between Chrysler and Daimler-Benz in May 1998 was only the latest manifestation of a trend that has seen one famous name after another disappear over the past two or three decades. But the apparent remorselessness of this trend blinded people to the fact that size could bring as many problems as solutions. Lured into the mainstream, all too many businesses found that they were being carried in the wrong direction; some sank without trace.

As Gary Hamel reminded readers of the *Financial Times* in April 1998: 'Size is not the ultimate competitive advantage. Just ask IBM,

McDonald's, General Motors or AT&T.' Innovation, says Hamel, is far more important than sheer size. He is absolutely right, not least because size can so easily inhibit innovation.

Demerger mania

Lured into the prevailing current of corporate acquisitiveness, people were forgetting the essential disciplines of business. They forgot how to stimulate growth organically. And, sure enough, what had once flowed suddenly began to ebb. Demerger mania took over. No sooner had the megamerger become a recurring headline than gigantic and apparently monolithic concerns like ICI began to move in the opposite direction, separating into businesses that had their own internal logic and were better able to plough their own furrows as free-standing concerns. As recession began to bite at the end of the 1980s, people began to pick up the Peters and Waterman mantra of 'sticking to your knitting', retreating to core competencies, and getting rid of the diversity that they had suddenly found they couldn't manage.

This wasn't the answer, either. After all, you can stick to your knitting, but what do you do when the yarn runs out? Single-minded knitters may be able to make progress for a while, specialising in doing one thing extremely well, but they are always liable to be rendered irrelevant by some competitor who can create an unexpected discontinuity or change the rules of the game. There is, however, one yarn that doesn't run out, and that, as we shall see in the coming chapters, is the customer relationship, provided you control that relationship.

Merger mania and demerger mania are still with us, sometimes dormant, but always liable to flare up without warning. They are the symptoms of a disease that is all too easy to catch when you are swimming in the business mainstream: that disease is faddism – and it has many manifestations. In management circles, we remember Business Process Re-engineering – sometimes known as downsizing. Beginning from a perfectly sensible impulse to control costs in order to survive recession, BPR became a horribly contagious fad. Soon, perfectly sensible people were seized with the bizarre notion that the only way to grow – organic growth being everyone's long-term aspiration – was to shrink. Then there was Total Quality Management – a fad par excellence. Nothing wrong with the idea of building in quality; it's just that in any well-run company it really ought to go without saying. TQM, which should have been a useful checking mechanism for middle manage-ment, became elevated to the level of corporate strategy, where it proved unduly labour-intensive, a barrier to the dynamic development of strategy. Enterprise Resource Planning belongs in the same bracket – not intrinsically a bad idea, but tending to create formulaic approaches that become barriers to clear and original thinking.

The real problems with fads is that people tend to follow them without thinking. Customer databases, for instance, are a good idea. But there comes a point when you have more information than you need, when too many of your staff are employed on tasks that have no real strategic value. Benchmarking is the last one I shall mention. Again, there is nothing intrinsically wrong with the idea of measuring yourself against the best, but it is hard to resist the tendency towards sameness. There is a semantic trap in expressions like 'industry standard', 'world-class' and 'best of breed'. They sound like worthy aspirations, but do you really want to be 'standard'? Are you happy to be classified? What does breeding have to do with anything? Corporate-speak of this kind makes people feel good; it makes them feel that they are doing the right thing; and it discourages them from thinking. Fads encourage you to swim in the mainstream, comparing yourself with your competitors, rather than thinking for yourself. Faddism is dangerous, because it is a substitute for imagination and creativity.

In the late 1990s, merger and demerger mania having died down, and many of the other fads having run their course, someone discovered parental advantage. Were you the best parent for this business you were buying, or was there a better parent somewhere else? If there was a better parent then you were hardly best placed to add shareholder value.

These second thoughts were difficult for a whole generation of executives who simply had no experience of expanding a company by themselves. Many of them had achieved all their significant successes by taking over other companies. Having done it once or twice, they would sit down and think: 'What else can I buy? If I don't have money I'll call the investment banker and he will find a way to finance it, maybe with shareholders' money . . .' It wasn't that such people were unintelligent. Far from it. Like business people down the ages, they had found a successful formula and tried to replicate it. In their own way, they were 'sticking to their knitting'. But their success rate was diminishing, and a lot found it hard to understand why – not least because they checked their behaviour against the current fads and couldn't see where they had gone wrong.

Today, the ambitious entrepreneur is no longer obsessed with finding the juiciest takeover targets. In certain areas, like privatised industries, regulation has made acquisition more difficult. Elsewhere, when a suitable candidate for takeover appears, the rumour mill begins to grind away and the price goes up. By the time you've done your sums and analyses, the company you were thinking of buying just isn't a bargain any more. While the takeover kings of the 1980s and 1990s are finding life harder as they face the new millennium, the real growth is being exhibited by small and medium-sized companies that have ignored what is happening in the mainstream and chosen instead to swim in their own little backwaters.

Backwaters, away from the hustle and bustle of the mainstream, are ideally suited to innovation – and thinking. Small fish can grow big there, particularly when there is venture capital floating around. In the mainstream, where publicly quoted companies battle for supremacy, no such sustenance is available. Silicon Valley in California was once a backwater, rapidly made prosperous by venture capitalists prepared to back people with knowledge, ideas and dynamism. By 1997, 75 per cent of the world's venture capital was flowing into Silicon Valley and the backwater had grown to the size of a great river. Its peculiar achievement has been to retain many of its original characteristics: the flexible regulatory environment, ferocious competition for talent, high personal rewards, culture of the hero-entrepreneur and availability of venture capital. I have used the term 'backwater' – although that seems inappropriate for Silicon Valley today – but 'microclimate' might be an equally apt metaphor for an environment in which the business life cycle is significantly faster. Hi-tech companies like Microsoft, Dell, Intel, Compaq and Sun Microsystems – all household names today – depended on venture capital in their developing years. So did Federal Express. Now biotechnology companies are making similar progress – often growing rapidly in their own backwaters or microclimates.

Changing competition

All the while, the competition has been changing. In the good old days – just a few decades ago – our competitors were rivals in our own industry, doing the same kinds of things that we were doing. These were people we could watch, people we knew by name, people about whom we knew a great deal. We could watch our competitor and when he did something we could react to that, in the sure knowledge that he would be doing the same. Sometimes you would gain an advantage, sometimes he would. But you were playing the same game, more or less according to the same rules.

What has changed today is that new competitors have entered the marketplace, people who don't play to the old rules. They don't think like you do, they don't know the industry as well as you do. More significantly, they don't have the vested interest in the game or the rules of the game that you have. Unconstrained by an existing mindset, or by physical assets, they are totally free agents – although sometimes it takes them a while to realise this. When Pepsi-Cola stepped up its challenge to the mighty Coca-Cola after World War II, it took time to discover that to make any headway, it had to change the rules. In the fifties, Pepsi spent millions of dollars studying new design, in the hope of coming up with something more marketable than the Coke bottle. But the 'swirl' bottle was no kind of breakthrough. It was only when the marketing genius John Sculley discovered that Pepsi's opportunity lay in the size of the package, not the design, that Pepsi began to make significant progress. When Pepsi launched larger, plastic bottles in the seventies, families responded by buying in bulk. Sculley became the company's president in 1977 at the tender age of 37, and ten years later he explained: 'Usually, you can only nullify a competitor's strength by changing the ground rules of the competition . . . If you can change the rules, you can often take a competitor's advantage by forcing him to move from his natural strengths.' *(Odyssey: Pepsi to Apple,* Sculley and Byrne, HarperCollins, 1994).

Even for the likes of Coca-Cola, to assume any kind of impregnability is potentially fatal in a world in which the life expectancy of the average organisation has shrunk to about ten years. Competition can be dangerous by being unpredictable. It can be even more dangerous by being invisible. Cruising along in the mainstream, you look around you and you think you know who your rivals are. But the rivals you can see are not your main threat. They are playing the same game, mostly following the same rules, being pulled along by the same current. It's the unknown competitor, lurking in a backwater somewhere, perhaps from another industry, who probably plays by completely different rules, who could make you irrelevant.

All these developments mean that the nature of change has changed – something to which hardly anyone has yet adjusted. Change is no longer continuous, no longer incremental. It has become discontinuous be-cause, when someone enters the market and changes the game in the process, that person has created a discontinuity. We have seen it repeatedly in recent years, and will see it more and more as technology makes it easier to translate a new strategy into action. The challenge is a dual one: first, to understand and take account of discontinuous change, then, ultimately, to be able to create your own discontinuity.

This is a daunting prospect – too daunting for some. Let's just consider the banks. For decades, even centuries, banks assumed their own indispensability. Was banking not one of the leading professions, alongside the church, the law, politics and medicine? Money, after all, was hardly likely to go out of fashion; surely people would always need bankers, just as they would always need doctors. Not necessarily.

The history of banks in the twentieth century provides evidence enough of the dangers of complacency. It is a history of institutions that have become increasingly sure of their longevity, with less and less reason. Secure in their privileged position, like big fish in the middle of the river, they built ever grander banking halls, ever more splendid headquarters buildings – temples to their own importance. When they suffered setbacks at the hands of competition, they tinkered with their products, offering different types of loans, even trespassing on the territory of mortgage banks or mutual and friendly societies by venturing into mortgages. If this did not work, they would be forced now and then to prune their workforce, close a few branches, or shut down some non-core part of their operation. With few exceptions, they failed utterly to make the most of their most precious asset – their customers. We shall examine this more closely in Chapter 5.

Suddenly, banks and insurance companies, thinking themselves secure in the mainstream of business, have found competitors emerging from the shallows, from obscure backwaters, or from other industry streams. Their astonishment was understandable. Who would have thought General Electric, a maker of aircraft engines and engineered plastics, would branch into financial services? Or that supermarkets selling washing powder and groceries would suddenly offer banking and insurance? It was perhaps more predictable that Richard Branson's Virgin empire would move into financial services with all the flair and agility of an organisation on the same wavelength as its customers. With Virgin, there are no great temples designed to impress and patronise customers, just accessible people primed to provide us with the products and services we are increasingly learning to demand.

What businesses are

The reality that today's successful businesses understand is that you are defined not by your product or service, but by the relationship you have with your customer, and the value you can create for that customer. In the past, people have found it sufficient that cigarette manufacturers make cigarettes, car manufacturers make cars, and banks look after your money. Not any more.

Nor is it enough simply to turn the focus away from the product and towards the customer. Loan-application forms, for instance, provide umpteen opportunities to ask questions of the customer. But are they the right questions? No doubt they provide plenty of useful information in the narrow context of loan approval. But do they give the bank the ability to anticipate the customer's needs? Almost certainly not. The trouble is that even the most comprehensive customer questionnaires will be able to cover only a limited amount of already well-trodden ground. Customers will respond from their own experience. No one asked for a Sony Walkman; no one asked for a mobile telephone; and no one asked for an in-car navigation system – but then no one imagined that a satellite would be able to monitor traffic jams anywhere from Bangkok to Buenos Aires.

Mastering the customer relationship is a lot more complicated than asking the right questions. It requires imagination, empathy and innovation – not qualities readily found in most large, comfortable businesses and corporations. For many executives, there is an ever-present temptation to wrap themselves in a comforting support structure that takes them further away from their customers – a potentially fatal mistake when success depends on taking control of the customer relationship. This is a theme we shall examine in greater detail in Chapter 5.

Creating discontinuity

The next big challenge is to create a discontinuity. Let's begin by defining terms. Cosmic scientists call it a singularity – a breakdown in the fabric of space and time. Black holes are an example, and their discovery has revolutionised astronomy.

Of course there is nothing new about discontinuity. History is littered with examples – wars, revolutions, inventions, social upheavals, all of which changed the way large numbers of people looked at the world. Earth, Ptolemy taught us, was the centre of the universe; and so we believed until Copernicus proved that Earth was just one of many planets in orbit round the sun. The laws of physics, Newton taught us, were rigid and immutable – until Einstein's Theory of Relativity taught us otherwise. Until Thomas Edison discovered the light bulb, it was universally assumed that artificial light could be generated only by oil or gas. This new source of light made any number of industrial processes possible, and changed the whole rhythm of ordinary people's lives. The personal computer and the Internet may be seen by future historians as similarly momentous discontinuities.

It would be tempting to say that, since the essence of these developments is their unpredictability, there is no point in worrying. But we are talking about a different kind of discontinuity.

The singularities or discontinuities of the past were mostly technical – inventions, in other words. They were created by scientists engaged in academic study. Business joined in at a later stage. Someone invented something, and the race began to exploit that invention. The race was won by the fastest, smartest competitor (never the inventor, of course, who hardly ever profited from his genius). And there was usually plenty of time for other competitors to join the race at a later stage.

The discontinuities of today often begin in the same way, with a technological breakthrough, although not necessarily. A technological breakthrough becomes a true discontinuity, changing the way business is conducted, only because it is planned and acted upon by that elite band of nimble companies and entrepreneurs with a speed that is liable to knock out most of the competition overnight. Look at Microsoft and the personal-computer revolution. Microsoft didn't wage a long and bloody war for supremacy against IBM. It made better decisions, supported by superior technology. The victory was won without any need for full-scale conflict.

Look at Rupert Murdoch and satellite broadcasting. His was a longer campaign, perhaps, but one distinguished by any number of surgical strikes – far-sighted deals that did not necessarily impress industry watchers at the time, but which secured Murdoch unique rights of access.

Satellite broadcasting was not Rupert Murdoch's idea. Sky Television was born in Europe in 1981, as Satellite Television plc, the brainchild of an English television producer named Brian Haynes. Haynes's vision was of a pan-European satellite-delivered TV service, first through cable systems and then eventually direct to dishes at home. By 1983, the system was beginning to work, with cable providers signed up in Holland, Belgium and other European countries; but Haynes's first £4 million of risk capital had gone and the next £6 million was tougher to find. Enter Rupert Murdoch, who paid an initial £10 million for a controlling interest in Satellite Television plc, renamed the channel Sky to give him a global link to his American Skyband satellite venture, and immediately set about enlarging his new acquisition.

Murdoch's ultimate success was achieved by such smart moves as circumventing British laws on cross-media ownership by broadcasting from the Luxembourg-based Astra satellite, outside British jurisdiction – while using his British newspapers to run promotional campaigns that no rival could possibly match. When it came to the fight to the finish with British Satellite Broadcasting, his key weapon was speed. For all that BSB promised better reception via its vaunted D-MAC system, Murdoch recognised that customers would buy only one system, and that would almost certainly be the first one available (provided it worked). From corporate launch to first broadcast in February 1989 took only eight months. But by that summer, with BSB still some way from getting on air, the satellite dishes were not moving fast enough for Murdoch's liking, and he decided on a relaunch, giving away thousands of dishes to carefully selected readers of his newspapers, launching Sky's own rental deal at the loss-leading price of £4.49 a week, and sending armies of unemployed double-glazing salesmen into the field.

Although Murdoch's costs were huge – he was particularly horrified at parting with £60 million for film rights – they were a fraction of BSB's. And, when these combined costs made a merger almost inevitable, the deal finally negotiated in November 1990 forced BSB to surrender far more, in recognition of the market position Sky had already acquired.

His rival started out with more money than he had, more staff, and probably better technology. Rupert Murdoch had agility, speed and single-mindedness. He had one more factor in his favour – what we might call his 'outsider' complex, a burning desire to show the complacent British establishment that he could outwit them. This was a man who despised the mainstream.

Or look at Banc One, the US bank that has created discontinuity after discontinuity in its industry. Banc One made the first technical breakthrough with Bank Americard, known today across the globe as Visa. Then it introduced automatic teller machines; then small, convenient branches in supermarkets.

What distinguishes operators like Microsoft, News Group and Banc One is that they had their eyes on discontinuities they were uniquely placed to exploit. They never simply allowed themselves to be carried along by the prevailing current. Others, like Richard Branson of Virgin, needed no technological breakthroughs, but created discontinuities purely by inspiration.

Although we may learn from studying the likes of Gates, Murdoch and Branson, few of us will have the opportunity to emulate them. But there is room for millions of smart operators to create their own discontinuities.

What smart operators do

Well-run, imaginatively led companies like Marks & Spencer have been creating all sorts of much smaller but nonetheless significant discontinuities over the past few decades. First, there was the move into food. What was a clothes retailer doing selling food? Grocers scoffed to begin with; then, when they realised the competition was serious, they were outraged. By the time they had got used to the idea, Marks & Spencer had created a new discontinuity, by selling pre-cooked meals, packaged with such skill and customer awareness that they shaped a new niche market. A new generation of consumers changed its habits. Instead of a weekly shop, with the traditional housewife cooking most evenings, recycling food as inventively as possible until the end of the week, the British began to buy M&S ready meals on their way home from work.

Other discontinuities have followed. Having persuaded many customers to open M&S accounts, the retailer suddenly transformed itself into a purveyor of financial services.

These are the kinds of discontinuities that are within the reach of any resourceful chief executive. The only limit is your own imagination. People who talk about 'sticking to their knitting' are simply guilty of a lack of imagination. Let's look instead at what smart operators do:

- They challenge industry conventions
- They challenge their own assumptions about the nature of their business
- They learn from others
- They create alternative pictures of the future
- They create new customer needs rather than merely satisfy existing ones.

We shall explore these themes in greater detail in later chapters.

The illusion of control

If you want to survive in the twenty-first century, you have no choice: you've got to learn to create a discontinuity, to go against the flow, or someone else will and you'll find yourself being swept along in the wrong direction. A handful of industry leaders seem to know it instinctively – but most chief executives don't. Even if they accept it, they have no idea where to start. This is hardly surprising, as there are no business schools in the world that teach it.

Classical strategy is little help because it is based on the idea that there is a future out there. You study history, analyse relevant current factors, build bubble diagrams, charts and tables, consider the market, identify opportunities, assess your options. You look forward, considering the potential threats and possible countermeasures. You make projections, based on a vision of the future that is more or less conventional, or at least culled from a generally received number of possibilities.

Such exercises are hopelessly irrelevant today. Useful though they were in times of continuity, now they are dangerous: they may persuade you to think you know where you're going, when actually you don't. Now this is really hard to accept. Most chief executives are control freaks, so how can we expect them to admit to an absence of control? Yet this is what they must do if they are to succeed in the twenty-first century.

There are as many futures as we are willing to dream. The new challenge is to choose the future you want. If you have the wherewithal and ambition to bring it to the present faster than your competitors can react, you've made them irrelevant, you've created a discontinuity. That's the name of the game.

The difficulty for many executives, intelligent and resourceful men and women though they may be, is that creating and dealing with discontinuities is uncharted territory. Imbued with the tenets of classical strategy, they assume that the future is a linear progression from the past. They see the future as a concept greater than ourselves: it doesn't exist yet, of course, but it is taken for granted that it exists as an objective concept, that it will arrive, and will in due course become history. The best we can do is to try to guess as closely as possible how it will turn out.

Unless you have already chosen your future, this kind of reasoning is not merely unreliable, but wrong. It suggests that there is a natural flow in the world of business; it invites you to join the mainstream.

We have discussed some of the dangers of the mainstream, such as faddism and complacency. But can you recognise these tendencies? Take this familiar piece of business advice: 'If it ain't broke, don't fix it.' Common sense, isn't it? No point in creating trouble for its own sake. We all know how annoying it is to have people fiddling with things that worked perfectly well before. But be on your guard. This is the wisdom of the mainstream, the subtle, insidious voice of complacency. Don't rock the boat, the same voice might say – and, if we're not natural trouble-makers, we usually don't.

'If it ain't broke, don't fix it.' Here is the danger of the mainstream, in one familiar expression. Because its true corollary is: 'If it *is* broke, you're too late.' Just because a business is not showing obvious signs of distress is no reason to assume that it is safe. Your most dangerous competitor, remember, is probably invisible. By this I mean that they may be working in a completely different industry but may be just about to have a brilliant idea and leap over traditional industry barriers, like the clothes retailer who becomes a grocer, the supermarket that turns into a bank, and so on. You can't afford to let your guard drop for a minute.

In the introduction, I invited you to open your mind. If it's still open, I hope you will read on. If you are seduced by the mainstream, if you recognise that you really prefer to go with the flow, then put this book down now. Most people are conformists, and have nothing to be ashamed of. Life would be unbearable if we were all nonconformists. Business leaders could hardly lead if no one were prepared to be led. But this book is aimed squarely at those who lead, or want to lead. And this is one matter on which there is no real choice. If you want to lead, you must resist the mainstream, and be prepared to go against the flow.

The penalty for failure

If you are in any doubt about the penalty for failure, consult *Fortune* magazine. In July 1998, *Fortune* looked back five years to the 125 'Cool Companies' it had picked as winners from the hi-tech sector. Although an investor in those 'Cool Companies' would have beaten market averages, there were notable failures too. As *Fortune* put it, 'no matter how cool their products, tech companies that don't stay on the cutting edge are doomed . . . timing is everything'. Take Medio Multimedia, which went broke two years after receiving *Fortune's* accolade. Tied to CD-ROM technology, Medio Multimedia became a victim of changes in multimedia software. In retrospect, we can see that, by allowing itself to be carried by the prevailing CD-ROM current, it lost its independence of action.

Silicon Graphics was another example, a 'Cool Company' in 1993 that fell victim to discontinuities created by others – in this case, cheaper microprocessors and the inroads made by Microsoft's Windows NT.

A look at some of the household names in *Fortune's* Top 100 of 1990 is also instructive. These were big fish in the middle of the river. But were they safe in the mainstream? History tells us otherwise. Within less than ten years, the fortunes of each of the following companies had taken a significant turn for the worse:

1 **Occidental Petroleum** (down from 16th to 142nd) failed to diversify sufficiently to avoid being hit by the drop in worldwide oil prices resulting from declining demand from Asia.

2 **Tenneco** (down from 26th to 217th), the packaging and automotive business, has suffered from excess inventories of paperboard and a slump in demand for replacement motor components.

3 **General Dynamics** (down from 44th to 366th) had a difficult decade in defence and computing. But the future, with a new submarine in demand, and back orders totalling $14 billion, looks more solid.

4 **Unocal** (down from 40th to 267th), the largest exploration and production company in the world, is particularly vulnerable to fluctuations in crude-oil and gas prices.

5 **Unisys** (down from 43rd to 244th), makers of mainframe computers, suffered severe losses in the mid-1990s. In September 1998 the company changed tack, updating its product line and redefining itself as a company of innovative people that provides up-to-date solutions and services. Time will tell whether Unisys has gone against the flow in time.

CHAPTER 2 – DIGEST

Defying the current

Key message:
Success is achieved by leaders who have the courage and vision to defy prevailing business currents, identify opportunities and go for them, changing the rules of the game to bring unlooked-for benefits to appreciative customers.

Why?
Because the last decade of the twentieth century has proved that discontinuity, rather than innovation pure and simple, is the key to success.

What?
- The value curve – marketing your way to the top
- Finding the conduit
- Changing the game
- Speed and innovation
- Anticipating customer needs

So what?
So take a good look at your customers and work out what they really want.

CHAPTER 2

Defying the current

The value curve

Today's chief executive faces a triple-choice question, as outlined in the introduction to this book. Are you content to take the easy option, allowing others to set the pace, and being purely reactive? If so, you are a victim – one who may survive for a while, but whose days are surely numbered. Are you smarter than that, an adapter, able to go against the flow, sufficiently nimble and well informed to adapt quickly to changes in the marketplace? Or are you a shaper, one who has what it takes to create a new game with a new set of rules, and oblige your competitors to play it your way?

You can measure yourself. In the curve overleaf, almost every business starts with saleable skills. Package those skills into products and you have the makings of a business. Apply those products to markets and you are halfway up the curve. With greater customer focus you move into the upper half, and, once you can reliably create value for those customers, then you are where you want to be, in a position to be a shaper.

This curve, with its five essential elements, is applicable to just about every business. You cannot afford to neglect any one element. If, for instance, you neglect to maintain skills, your products will inevitably

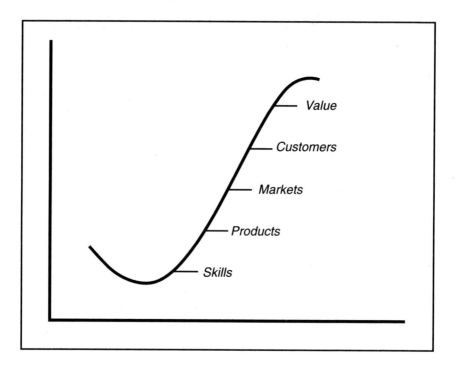

The value curve

suffer, your markets will decline, and you will have no hope of creating the customer value to which you may once have aspired.

Now let's look at how successful companies have created or harnessed discontinuities to their advantage, how they have defied the prevailing currents and chosen their own route to the future. There could be no better starting point than Microsoft, the company that dominates the business world as we enter the new millennium.

'We set the standard' is Microsoft's motto, and it says much about the business philosophy that drives Bill Gates. Independence of mind has been the secret of his success. While other companies played to what they thought were their strengths, developing outstanding products, then honing those products to new levels of excellence, Microsoft played a strategic game of being in the right place at the right time, of anticipating trends, of trying to understand what customers would really want a few years hence. Refusing to view its competitors as rivals, Microsoft avoided confrontation. It was happy to form alliances wherever there was a possibility of mutual benefit. While his competitors struck exclusive deals with their chosen hardware suppliers, Gates kept his options open, dealing with several different hardware suppliers. In retrospect, we can see that one of his key tactics was never to do anything that might suck him into the industry's mainstream and restrict his freedom to exploit the latest trend in computer technology. Microsoft finished up in the mainstream, of course, but it was a current largely of its own making.

Business genius though his record clearly reveals him to be, Gates is by no means the great innovator of his industry. That title should, perhaps, belong to Steve Jobs and Apple. But let's look again at the value curve and we can see that Apple never really got beyond the skills and products stages. They had a superb product, no doubt about that. The Macintosh was infinitely more versatile than the basic PC; Apple's designers, programmers and computer geniuses did themselves more than justice. But they never mastered the mass marketing of their product. Despite having created a brand-new game, Apple allowed Microsoft to write the rule book. Eventually, despite starting out as a shaper, Apple fell into the category of victim.

In this chapter we will consider not only the famous few – Microsoft, Virgin, News International and other headline makers of the last decade of the twentieth century – but also organisations of varying shapes and sizes that satisfied each of the following requirements:

- Find a conduit – the user's means of access
- Change the rules of the game
- Act quickly and exploit innovation
- Control and manage the customer relationship

We shall examine each of these in turn.

Find the conduit

In the competition between Apple and Microsoft, the crucial contest was to find the conduit – the user's means of access. As the competition intensified, it became clearer and clearer that this was a race for ubiquity in which the winner would take all. Whose technology would be within everyone's reach? Accessibility would be everything. And this was a desperately one-sided contest, because, for all the skill of its people, Apple never really grasped what was at stake.

In this case, the conduit was the operating system, and Apple's big mistake was that it pursued a proprietary-systems strategy rather than the open-systems approach used by Microsoft. Apple insisted on its computers having their own operating system, and did not make that operating system available to other manufacturers. Microsoft, by contrast, developed the DOS operating system, then made it universally available. Crucially, Gates persuaded industry giants such as IBM to make DOS the standard. By the time the Apple Mac should have been sweeping aside the competition, users or would-be users found that it was incompatible with everyone else's PC.

Microsoft's other great rival, of course, was IBM, and Gates was always determined that his new operating system should not be exclusive to IBM. Under the terms of the contract that his lawyers negotiated with IBM, Microsoft was permitted to sell the operating system to other companies and to consumers – an opportunity that was therefore expressly denied to IBM. At the time, of course, hardly anyone on either side could imagine the immense significance of the deal, and the extent to which it would work in Microsoft's favour. As far as IBM were concerned, Gates was developing an operating system for their computer, and what he did with it afterwards was immaterial. Microsoft's detractors imply some kind of manipulation or deceit behind some of their more spectacular coups, but there is no reason to believe that IBM's attorneys were deliberately deceived. They, like everyone else, simply did not guess that an entire industry would emerge based on hardware and software compatible with the IBM PC.

The next crucial series of events occurred in late 1988, when Microsoft was approached by IBM executives who wanted to have another try at cracking the home PC market. Gates suggested a multimedia machine – an integrated CD-ROM drive and sound card. IBM spotted an opportunity to restore market confidence in its ability to lead the industry and eagerly set about designing such a machine for use in the home. Gates assigned a twenty-six-year-old Yale graduate, Rob Glaser, to be his principal adviser on the project. Glaser, apart from proving an inspirational salesman, made a suggestion of immense strategic significance. He suggested that Microsoft launch a 'virtual standard' for multimedia that could be used in all IBM-compatible personal computers, not just IBM's. Gates was quick to give the green light.

As we know, Gates had wanted his operating system to be available to as many users as possible – not least because he was unsure whose hardware would prevail in the long term – and this strategy was triumphantly vindicated. By 1989 DOS accounted for 66 per cent of the market. Windows was designed to run on DOS, and, when this new system came into widespread operation, it rapidly achieved total dominance of its market. By 1991 a leading software journal was moved to declare: 'Microsoft is now driving the industry, not IBM.' Microsoft had forced a generation of software developers to conform to its standards. Bill Gates had won by doing it his way, by defying the current that had sustained IBM and Apple.

Early connoisseurs of video technology will recall a similar battle for the effective monopoly of video-systems supply between the Betamax system developed by Sony and Video Home Systems (VHS) developed by a rival consortium led by JVC. The Betamax, independent experts almost unanimously agreed, was a superior product, and most of the technical innovations were Sony's. But it lost the battle. Why? For the simple reason that its rival gradually acquired the crucial control over the customer relationship. This was a step-by-step process. The first and most crucial step was that in 1976 JVC developed a machine that doubled Sony's recording time of one hour. As a result of this one innovation, which gave VHS a vital edge in terms of the access key/platform, RCA joined the VHS camp, and a price-cutting strategy began, which hurt Sony. At the same time, VHS was pouring resources into buying feature films, which was what most customers wanted. Within five years VHS had begun to overtake its rival, and, when the magazine *Video Today* warned its readers that the VHS selection would henceforth be 'slightly broader', the writing was on the wall for Sony. One crucial innovation, greater customer focus and, over the period, greater determination to pursue a chosen strategy, won the day for VHS, and turned an adapter into a shaper.

In the world of modern technology, the conduit is the most essential ingredient – regardless of whether you create that conduit yourself or use an existing one. By comparison, the quality of product is a relatively minor consideration. Consider telecommunications. Countless businesses have been launched and have prospered by using the existing telephone network. Insurance, once a form of business conducted face-to-face, is now administered overwhelmingly by phone, and companies like Direct Line insurance in the UK have wiped the floor with long-established companies by simply exploiting that conduit more quickly, while giving better value to the customer.

In the 1980s, the French government, intoxicated with the success of its information-technology industry, launched Minitel, an ingenious TV screen accessible via the telephone network. The idea was to create a revolutionary new business tool, available to anyone in France, that would enable them to shop, trade and strike deals with a speed that would be the envy of the rest of the world. To this end, and to ensure that the state retained control of the project, the government supplied Minitel screens free of charge. Technically, the Minitel was a brilliant product – but there were two vital weaknesses. First, it was incompatible with foreign telephone networks, making it useless for exporters, importers or anyone wishing to look beyond France's borders. And secondly, it was about to be overtaken by the Internet. Now that the same business users can do unlimited business via the Internet, Minitel's days are numbered – and the French government undone by the kind of arrogance that saw IBM fall so suddenly from its lofty perch. For two reasons, both of which should have been apparent to any far-sighted executive, Minitel had chosen the wrong conduit.

If we look ahead, it is clear that the Internet and the World Wide Web offer the ideal conduit for many thousands of emerging businesses. But that will be of little use if the business concerned neglects the three other vital factors.

Change the game

VHS and Microsoft, in their different ways, have changed the lives of millions of people; they have created discontinuities that can reasonably be mentioned alongside the printing press, the light bulb, the personal computer and the Internet. And yet, since neither started out with the best product in its field, it is certainly arguable that their success was not in the long-term interests of the consumer. From a business perspective, that's just too bad. The point is that, although they did not invent the new game, they changed the rules and gradually made the game their own.

We have talked about changing the rules, or nature, of the game, and when it comes, literally, to games – sport, in other words – there is no shortage of outstanding examples, where independence of mind and a willingness to defy the prevailing current can bring unexpected rewards.

Of all the triumphs of the great heavyweight boxer Muhammad Ali, none was more remarkable than his comeback victory in Zaïre (now the Democratic Republic of Congo) over the gigantic George Foreman, a man who had demolished Ali's old rival Joe Frazier to claim the world title. Realising after two rounds that he could not outpunch the formidable Foreman, Ali performed his now-legendary 'rope-a-dope' routine. To the amazement and dismay of watching commentators, he abandoned his trademark 'Ali shuffle', made little or no attempt to escape Foreman's murderous punches, and huddled against the ropes, inviting Foreman to hit him. While Ali protected himself as well as he could, taking most of the blows on his arms, he taunted Foreman incessantly, urging him to hit harder. His extraordinary strategy was triumphantly vindicated six rounds later, by which time an infuriated Foreman had punched himself to the point of exhaustion, and was knocked out by Ali's sudden flurry of retaliation.

Another sporting example is perhaps more instructive, for it perfectly illustrates the ability to create a discontinuity, to play a game in a completely different way, in response to a new set of rules. In rugby union, each team of fifteen is divided into eight forwards – traditionally huge, strong men – and seven backs, who are traditionally fast and skilful handlers of the ball. For decades, the strong men would push, wrestle and jump to win the ball, before feeding it back to the backs to run, kick or pass it. At times, particularly when rain made handling difficult, the game could settle into a sterile trial of strength between two sets of forwards, with backs merely kicking for position. As international rugby turned from an amateur to a professional game, and became more aware of its commercial potential after the 1991 World Cup, the authorities decided to change the rules to make the game faster and more entertaining.

The most significant change was that they made it illegal to handle the ball on the ground: whenever a player was brought to ground, he was obliged to release the ball instantly. Suddenly there was a new emphasis on handling skills, even among the forwards. Increasingly, the challenge was to recycle the ball quickly, to pass it from hand to hand. It took time for most teams to adjust – but not the New Zealand All Blacks. Under their coach, Laurie Mains, they revolutionised their style of play. Forwards were given new regimes; they had to be fitter and faster; instead of practising pushing and wrestling, they practised handling the ball. Traditional strong men lost out to more athletic types. The backs, conversely, had to become more physical; they concentrated on tackling, and breaking tackles. The aim was simple: to play a true fifteen-man game in which any player, anywhere on the field, could win the ball in a tackle, run with it, commit opponents, then pass to a teammate capable of carrying on the attack. Ironically, continuity was the new name of the game in rugby – yet in our terms, by virtue of its defiance of the prevailing current, this was a classic *dis*continuity.

Most opponents wilted before the All Blacks' all-round attacking game, conceding final scorelines more appropriate to games of basketball. Although the All Blacks narrowly lost the 1995 World Cup Final to an inspired host nation, South Africa, they dominated world rugby for the next three years, losing only two of their next forty-one games – true shapers in their field, to whose standards every other rugby nation had to adapt.

The game, for our purposes, is your mission, your job – what you add. And it is crucial that you do not define yourself too narrowly. It may be clear enough if you are a lawyer, doctor, carpenter or plumber – although even then it is perfectly feasible for carpenters or plumbers to turn themselves into home-improvement consultants/practitioners. But, when you are a large company or corporation, definition becomes an important issue. Disney, for instance, doesn't just make films, or run amusement parks. Disney's game is a much broader one, which involves selling fantasy, emotion, aspiration, family values, even redemption. What makes it more complicated is that Disney itself provides only half. The rest comes from the customer, because the Disney experience happens, above all, in the customer's brain. We shall return to this theme in Chapter 5.

Having created its own game, Disney is the exception. Most operators are playing a game that others have played before. The challenge for them is to play it better than anyone else, and that usually involves reinterpreting, bending or changing the rules in order to create uniqueness or discontinuity. Often, external forces bring about a change in the rules, and when this happens the winners are those that transform themselves first. Lord King realised as much when British Airways, the formerly state-run airline, was suddenly let loose in the world of global competition at the instigation of Prime Minister Margaret Thatcher.

Before Lord King was appointed chairman in 1981, to prepare the airline for privatisation, BA was said by its detractors to stand for 'Bloody Awful'. Over the ensuing eleven years its image underwent a revolution, as it proceeded to live up to its new slogan of 'The World's Favourite Airline'. Tough decisions were taken in the years leading up to privatisation in 1987: there were heavy staff cuts, unprofitable routes were suspended and surplus assets disposed of. The airline had recorded a deficit of £544 million in the financial year 1981– 2. By the time BA was privatised, its shares were eleven times oversubscribed. Freed from the constraints of government ownership, BA merged with British Caledonian in July 1987 and the basic transformation was complete.

But it was over the next six years that BA really showed the rest of the world what it could do by providing a new level of customer service. In 1988 new Club World (longhaul business-class) and Club Europe (short-haul premium-class) brands were introduced, with a new First Class service the following year. When the Club Europe lounge opened at Heathrow in 1991, it was the largest business-class lounge in Europe, and within three years BA had fourteen Club Europe lounges. Nowadays, business travellers take it for granted that they will not have to hang about in crowded waiting areas, tripping over children and luggage while inhaling other people's cigarette smoke; but it was BA that pioneered the lounges. By changing customer expectations, BA had changed the rules of the game.

Air Miles, a points-earning system valued even more by holiday-makers than business travellers, was another BA innovation. Introduced in 1988 in partnership with Shell and NatWest, it enabled customers of those two organisations to enjoy free flights once they had notched up a certain number of points. Ten years on, Shell and NatWest were still involved, and Air Miles had been extended to BA's own frequent flyers as well as customers of many other organisations. In 1998, Air Miles was a fully owned BA subsidiary with a turnover in excess of £150 million and its customer-services centre was receiving an average of 15,000 calls a day. This was a classic discontinuity, creating a new game with new rules.

Microsoft achieved something similar, not only by developing a new conduit, as we have seen, but also by gambling that consumers would be willing to spend extra money on a multimedia-equipped machine. Bill Gates and his colleagues were convinced that despite the 'couch-potato' image of a mass of the population, they would be able to persuade a sufficient number to do something more constructive with their time.

In those days, 20 million television sets were sold in the United States every year, compared with just 1.4 million PCs. The closest equivalent to the home computer was a Nintendo video-game machine – which came without a keyboard, memory or additional processing power. Gates was convinced that multimedia encyclopedias, health guides and travel planners were some of the future titles that would have broad appeal. He hoped that passive sensationalism wasn't the last word in home entertainment. And he was right.

In other industries, the game has changed through a process of evolution. When computers, for instance, were in their infancy, the game was about selling hardware – shifting as many boxes as possible. Different kinds of software were created primarily for the purpose of selling more hardware. The game changed as the computers themselves became more of a commodity, and the crucial difference came to be what the software enabled you to do with them. The new game was selling solutions – and, to begin with, that required intermediaries, experts with the specialist knowledge to guide their clients towards buying the right machines with the software that did the things they needed. Now this particular game has changed as globalisation has made that knowledge more widely available. With suppliers able to make their case directly to clients, the intermediaries are being squeezed, and the game has moved on from selling solutions to being an integrator, and selling advice.

Adapting to a changing game can often mean rethinking your entire approach to business. *Encyclopaedia Britannica* provides a striking example. For decades the business had depended on the idea that people could be persuaded to part with around £2000 for an unparalleled knowledge resource. Encyclopedia salesmen may have been the butt of jokes for generations, but few could quarrel with the remarkable success achieved by the *Britannica* since World War Two. Not just academic institutions or rich individuals but ordinary people, particularly families, were persuaded to part with this substantial sum of money – often the equivalent of several months' salary – on the grounds that this would be a precious source of knowledge for everyone in the house. High-pressure salesmanship and ingenious payment schemes were the main tools. But the development of computers and the approach of the Internet made it clear that *Britannica* could never survive into the twenty-first century on the same basis.

Faced with Microsoft's electronic *Encarta* encyclopedia – by no means as comprehensive as *Britannica* but sufficient for many people's purposes – *Britannica* had to rethink its entire business strategy. The solution was to switch from selling £2000 units to selling units in CD-ROM form – at a mere 5 per cent of the previous unit price. Few people within the organisation could understand how it could possibly achieve profit-ability in this way. And, of course, most of the sales force had to go. Instead, *Encyclopaedia Britannica* employed teams of researchers and editors to work on updating the material day by day. The result, amazingly, is that *Britannica* is profitable again, with many more satisfied customers now able to draw much more easily on a still-unrivalled volume of knowledge, which they can update whenever they want.

Act quickly and exploit innovation

A willingness to innovate is a necessary condition of any business that aims to go against the flow. But there are two ways of innovating: you can have a new idea, or you can use an existing idea in a new way – which can often be the less risky and more lucrative option. And you must act quickly. Cable News Network (CNN) is an outstanding example of the first kind. Since Ted Turner launched CNN on 1 June 1980, the public has been introduced to the concept of rolling news coverage. There have been many occasions when CNN have been the only broadcasters to carry a particular story – and their judgement is endorsed by viewing figures of 800 million in 210 countries.

During the Gulf War of 1991, millions of viewers heard the voices of the CNN reporters broadcasting the breaking news – still CNN's trade-mark. In this case three reporters, Bernard Shaw, John Hollingworth and

Peter Arnett, were filmed reporting from underneath a table in their Baghdad hotel room on the US air assault on the Iraqi capital.

Even the *Larry King Live* show is full of innovation. Seen as the McDonald's of political discourse, it is an example of direct-contact TV, easy to handle for the politicians, with questioning not as probing as that to be found with, say, Jeremy Paxman at the BBC. Bill Clinton appeared on the Larry King show no fewer than sixteen times during the 1992 election. King's show is the only talk show where viewers from all over the world are invited to telephone the show's politicians and celebrities with questions. In May of 1998 King happily signed up with CNN into the next millennium.

Recent innovations include CNN Interactive, the first network to use the complementary nature of television and the Internet and create a new form of news coverage. By leveraging CNN's worldwide news-gathering organisation of more than 3500 news specialists in 32 bureaux and more than 700 broadcast affiliates worldwide, CNN Interactive delivers the most comprehensive, breaking global and US news and events coverage on the Internet today. CNN is forever looking to break new ground, and in 1998 it launched the CNN African Journalist of the Year award, to promote the recognition of journalistic excellence in Africa. But, as other rivals like the BBC enter the market for 24-hour news, CNN is struggling to hold on to market share.

Probably even more important than innovation itself is a readiness to exploit innovation – which is by no means the same thing. As we have already observed, it's not usually the inventor who makes a fortune, but the person who builds a business on that invention. The key here is speed – and luck.

When Netscape developed the first Internet browsers, it appeared momentarily that the world of IT lay at this young company's feet. Move aside, Microsoft. Hail the new arrival. But Microsoft was too smart, and, above all, too quick. While Netscape was still promising the Earth,

Microsoft developed its own browser and gave it a prominent place on the desktops of its latest Windows software. Millions of consumers bought computers with Microsoft's software and Internet browser already installed. Netscape caught a sudden cold. Whatever the outcome of the US government's lawsuit against Microsoft, there was a simple lesson in this sudden reversal of fortune: you must move faster than your competitor can react.

Let's move for a moment down the scale of enterprise and look at the world of personal organisers – those pocket-sized pieces of computer technology as indispensable to the modern executive as the Filofax was in the late 1970s and early 1980s. The first personal organisers were slow and bulky, and it was several years before the products became genuinely user-friendly. The one that emerged on top as the millennium hove into view was the Palm Pilot, made by Palm Computing, a division of US Robotics, which was later acquired by 3Com, the California-based computer-networking business. And the crucial element in the Palm Pilot's success was timing.

The Palm Pilot was the brainchild of the Cornell graduate and former Intel employee Jeff Hawkins. But Hawkins did not get it right first time. His first attempt, the Zoomer, was, as he confessed to the magazine *Fast Company* in June 1998, 'the slowest computer ever made by man . . . too big and too expensive'. His great good fortune was that in August 1993 he was beaten into the marketplace by the Newton – Apple's pet project on which the company ultimately spent $500 million before abandoning it four and a half years later. The Newton had all the same failings as the Zoomer, and took the brunt of critical opprobrium. Hawkins was able to secure financial backing for a second attempt, and this time he got it right.

It wasn't easy. The problem was that while everyone agreed that a personal organiser should be small enough to fit in a shirt pocket, everyone also agreed that it needed to be smart enough to recognise different forms of handwriting. This meant creating a complicated software program – which would inevitably make the machine either bigger or slower. And there was one more thing on which everyone was agreed: this machine must be capable of being operated by anyone after only the most cursory reading of the instructions. Hawkins's answer was to go against the flow, and insist that he could create a desirable product only by requiring users to master a new method of handwriting. To the astonishment of many of his colleagues, Hawkins developed Graffiti, an ingenious handwriting code requiring each letter to be composed by a single stroke, without lifting the pen from the screen: many letters remained unchanged, but an A, for instance, was written as an inverted V and an F as an inverted L. Even his colleagues, many of whom had considered it commercial suicide to demand so much from the customer, changed their tune when they discovered how easy the system was to master. The rest is history. Within eighteen months of launch, the Palm Pilot had shipped more than a million units, making it the fastest-selling computer product ever, the heart of an industry, with more than 5000 programmers working on new software applications. The stage is set for a trial of strength with Microsoft, which is apparently determined to enter the market with software based on its Windows CE system. Jeff Hawkins and Palm Computing were not shapers in the sense that they created the market. But they went against the flow at a crucial moment, and made the quantum leap required of a successful twenty-first-century business, refining their product to the point where it is, for the moment at least, in blissful control of its customer relationship. At such a point of market dominance, you are entitled to call yourself a shaper.

All innovators must take risks. If you go against the flow, you are bound to fail now and again. A salmon, in its journey upriver, will often fail with its first attempt to leap a waterfall. But it will not be daunted. A willingness to fail is one of the prerequisites for success.

The Beatles, the most popular pop group of all time, were supreme risk-takers, forever curious to discover new sound. A list of revolutionary concepts includes: fade-ins; mid-song silences; sitars (all firsts, but commonplace today); backwards accompaniment; and even cutting up sections of song, throwing the pieces in the air and sticking them back together. It was their constant invention that led the group to seventeen number-one singles in a row.

Richard Branson has always been similarly unafraid of failure – and, contrary to the impression he sometimes conveys of being a man with a Midas touch, he has had his fair share of failures. He started a London listings magazine called *Event*, which was a failure. Virgin Cola has been, to say the least, a disappointment. And, ever since Britain's railways were privatised in 1994, Virgin Trains have been as widely reviled as any of the private operators on that benighted network. There have been other failures, but they have been comfortably outnumbered by successes.

Branson's successes have been firmly based on his determination to go against the flow. By his own account, when he decided to go into the personal-financial-services market, a lot of people said: 'Whatever for? It's a dreary, discredited business.' To which he replied, 'Yeah, that's why.' He has certainly made a success of some unpromising material. Virgin's company brochure puts it like this: 'Virgin's target markets are often those where the customer has been consistently ripped-off or under-served, where confusion reigns and the competition is complacent.' And, for all the variety of Virgin's ventures, hundreds of other ideas and possibilities have been rejected. According to Virgin, 'Nine out of ten projects we look at are potentially very profitable but, if they don't fit in with our values, we reject them.' One of those values seems to be enjoyment – brilliantly communicated by Branson himself, of course, but also acted upon throughout his companies. This brings us to the last of our four requirements for those determined to defy the current.

Control and manage the customer relationship

Whereas in many stores customers quickly get badgered and harried by store personnel, the complete opposite is the philosophy at Virgin stores, in particular their spectacular Megastores. Virgin know that the products they're selling are great. That is the same with many other stores, but their cutting edge is that Virgin stores are also great places to be – places 'where people go to just while away the time'. That's just fine by Virgin: 'Today's browser is tomorrow's customer.'

Above all, Richard Branson has taken the trouble to empathise with his customers. To ensure that he experiences what they experience, he turns up in unexpected places, whether it be flying his own flights (sometimes dressed as a steward), telephoning his own switchboards (with deliberately tricky queries) or constantly questioning his customers on how they could be served better. The key is to jettison the conventional notion that you are a provider of a certain kind of product or service, and that all you can do is refine that product or service to the best of your ability.

The key to the remarkable success of Virgin Atlantic Airways – winning awards for best transatlantic airline and best business class for six successive years – is that Branson has used his creativity and imagination to ensure that it's not just a good price that his carrier offers. Unless you travel Virgin Atlantic as frequently as once a month, you can almost guarantee that Branson will have come up with another gimmick to keep the passenger coming back for more next time. He never rests on his laurels. Although his once-excellent food-and-amenity kits now seem ordinary, regular travellers will keep coming back because all Branson has done is put the cash in other places.

Disregarding the conventional belief that airline passengers are passive victims who simply require cosseting with the best possible food, hot towels and pretty, smiling stewardesses, Branson has tried to empower customers. Branson understood before his rivals that on long-haul flights there is a never-ending battle against boredom; if he can relieve boredom and allow his clientele greater choice, they will be duly appreciative. In Virgin Upper Class – the best business-class yet, according to most transatlantic business travellers – Branson has offered manicure and massage, a 'snoozezone' for passengers who simply want to sleep; on the ground, he offered passengers in a hurry a lift on the back of a motorbike into central London. Virgin's business-class lounge opened at Heathrow in 1993 with standard faxes, bar and showers, and even a library.

On any Virgin transatlantic flight you now have a choice of at least eight movies, a further variety of TV and audio channels, plus Nintendo and PC games. Even the safety video, featuring cartoon characters with well-known voice-overs, gets more contented chuckles in its three-minute run than some supposedly comic feature films.

In the mid-1990s, Virgin having rubbed off some of its lustre, BA realised it had to reinvent itself again. Since 1994 it has introduced a number of new features to meet the goal of 'delighting customers'. These include telephone check-in on short-haul flights, a 'raid-the-larder' facility at any time of night on long-haul flights, new tilting seats that offer a further degree of comfort and ergonomic support, and head rests with 'ears' that support your head whichever way you sleep. The new catchphrase is 'speed on the ground, space in the air'. The new mission, enunciated in 1997, is 'to be the undisputed leader in world travel'. Underlying all of BA's success is the motivation and commitment of employees, 87 per cent of whom are now shareholders. Keeping them motivated is not so simple, however, as we shall see in later chapters.

Knowing your customer – whether your customer is another business or the actual consumer makes no difference – is essential. This doesn't mean simply asking customers what they want, then trying to give it to them. It means getting to know your customers so that you can *anticipate* what they will want. This requires a level of imagination and empathy not found in the average executive. It requires, at the very least, an instinct for human psychology; a degree in the subject would be no bad thing.

Customer awareness of this kind can be proved at any level – as Nicolas, the wine merchant, showed me in London recently. I was looking round the shop, contemplating a purchase or two, when I noticed a man come in and buy several bottles with labels that seemed to be no more than coloured paper. Then I noticed where he had got them from – a stack of bottles, distinguished from one another simply by the fact that some had red labels, some blue, some yellow and some green.

I asked the manager to explain. Just colour-coding, he said. One colour signified a soft and fruity wine, another more earthy and tannic, and so on. Many of his customers, he explained, knew very little about wine, and could not tell the difference between one label and another; above all, they had no way of knowing whether a given wine, regardless of price, was the kind of wine they would like. But, once they knew that the yellow label signified a particular type of wine, they would come back and buy that one time and again.

How very sensible and customer-friendly to classify wines according to their obvious characteristics and explain these to the customer! Why should wine drinkers be obliged to study their subject in depth in order to enjoy the product? In London at least, Nicolas has defied the prevailing current of wine snobbery and provided true customer value – and seems to be prospering as a result.

Kinepolis, a Belgian operator of cinema complexes, took a different kind of gamble with its customers in the mid-1990s. Noting that the typical Belgian was reducing cinema-going from eight visits a year to just two, Kinepolis decided to challenge the conventional wisdom that cinema had ceased to be a mass entertainment medium, and was confined to sophisticated audiences in city centres. The Kinepolis megaplex had 700 seats instead of the typical 100, screens that were more than three times as large, 70mm projection instead of the ubiquitous 35mm and – the killer touch, this – moved out of the city centre into the suburbs, where they could offer free parking. Within a single year, Kinepolis had won 50 per cent of market share in Brussels, while expanding the cinema-going market by no less than 40 per cent.

In a world where customers have more and more access to an ever more bewildering variety of products, whether in information techno-logy, wine or filmed entertainment, the prize will belong – and deservedly so – to those businesses that offer genuine help to the searcher for value. The first essential is to identify your preferred customer. The accompanying diagram shows the prime customer con-siderations of time and money. Although there are opportunities at the lower end of the market, most businesses will choose, in the words of

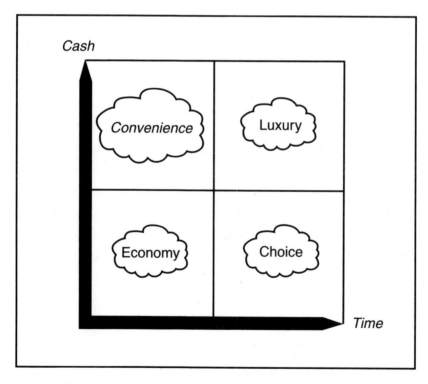

Customer demands: the time and money quadrant

the Watergate investigators Woodward and Bernstein, to 'follow the money'. That means concentrating on the top half. In the top right-hand corner of the quadrant lie the diminishing band of people who are cash-rich and time-rich – probably through having inherited large amounts of money. These are the target customers for private banks and makers of luxury goods. Businesses in this area offer exclusivity, or snob value.

The most promising area for most businesses, and the one with the most rapidly growing clientele, is the top left corner, representing the customer who is cash-rich and time-poor – high achievers with high material expectations, but little time to devote to shopping. This is where we shall concentrate our investigations.

One approach to the cash-rich, time-poor customer is the one-stop shop, where the prime value is convenience. Wal-Mart is an outstanding example, a store that defied the prevailing retail currents by mixing up different kinds of goods traditionally bought in totally different types of store. The received wisdom was that, if a shopper went in search of luxury cosmetics, that shopper would go to a completely different part of town from the shopper in search of practical household goods – mops, oven cleaners and light bulbs.

Wal-Mart took the view that different types of goods didn't necessarily attract entirely different types of customers, and, if you offered people an opportunity to buy electronic equipment and groceries, stationery and medicines, DIY tools and cosmetics, at the same time, most would happily do so – provided they felt they were getting good value. And Wal-Mart had no ties to the brands it sold; it was clearly independent, so customers did not feel they were being manipulated. Rather, they were being offered the opportunity to buy an unbeatable range of quality goods at unbeatable value, all in one store – the comprehensive one-stop shop.

Gary Hamel, although a Wal-Mart admirer, has made the point that, for all the stores' massive economies of distribution, you can waste hours searching for something like a can-opener, so that any saving is liable to be wiped out by the cost of searching. Hamel prefers to look for search economies via the Internet, ordering goods and having them delivered to his home. Given that so many people are accustomed to climbing into their cars to head off for a day's entertainment – incorporating shopping, the cinema, a meal and who knows what else – I suspect it may be a while before Internet shopping grips the mass of the population. I do believe, however, that the era of the cyber-broker will shortly be upon us – and the shapers, and winners, will be those who defy the prevailing currents in retailing, and offer to save customers time and money by sifting information and identifying best products and services for particular customers, thereby providing a new kind of value.

Another retailing gambit has been cross-selling – based on the idea that, once you have a customer hooked into buying one product, you should be able to persuade him to buy another. Cross-selling can work, if the secondary product is of equivalent quality, or equally appropriate to the customer in question, and if the seller's operation is sufficiently co-ordinated.

Dick Kovacevich, chief executive of Wells Fargo, built his reputation on cross-selling, in an industry with a less-than-inspiring record in this area. Kovacevich was one of the first bankers to recognise that banking is a form of retailing – so much so that he insists that Wells Fargo should not have branches, but 'stores'. He built his own reputation by building Norwest, now a subsidiary of Wells Fargo, into one of the ten biggest banks in the US. At Norwest, Kovacevich encouraged his staff to build relationships with their customers and sell them as many financial products as possible. By clever, targeted cross-selling, Norwest managed to increase sales by 15 per cent a year between 1988 and 1998 – described by the *Financial Times* as 'an astonishing rate compared with the performance of its peers'.

Elsewhere, banks have tried to cross-sell financial products, but with-out the organisation to help the customer manage the portfolio. The result is rapid disillusionment – as I and several of my KPMG colleagues have discovered when we need to transfer accounts to another country. At the very moment when your bank should be trying to help you cope with a professional upheaval, they insist that you make umpteen different telephone calls to deal with your current account, your savings account, your mortgage, and the equity investments you made at the suggestion of their own 'personal financial adviser'. It is at moments like these that customers realise that all the different products they have bought have been purely for the convenience of the retailer, and not for their (the customer's) convenience at all.

Bundling – the latest term for persuading people to buy more than one thing from the same source – is different, because it is customer-focused, and offers to save the customer trouble. It can be combined with the one-stop shop, so that, for instance, if you're going to stop your car to refuel, you may well want to refuel yourself at the same time – and buy some tapes for the car radio, maybe food for dinner when you get home, plus a bit of spending money in case you go out later, plus a magazine, and so on. Hence the transformation of garages with petrol pumps into miniature – or sometimes even full-size – supermarkets. We shall discuss bundling in greater detail in Chapter Four.

CHAPTER 3 – DIGEST

What's stopping you?

Key message:
Every organisation has structures and systems that make it hard to change. But look at those obstacles afresh and you will see that they are the best tools you have to work with – your levers of change.

Why?
Because, if you don't learn to switch your levers to ON, your potential for growth will wither away.

What?
The seven levers of change:
- Strategy – make the future your own
- People – capability, motivation and opportunity
- Process – building in efficiency, quality and effectiveness
- Structure – and why it can only disable
- Culture – identity, ritual, stories and symbols
- Technology – make sure it doesn't restrict your vision
- Products and Services – bridging the customer's frustration gap

So what?
So reprogramme your organisation by realigning your levers of change.

CHAPTER 3

What's stopping you?

However determined you are to embark on a brave new strategy for your company, the chances are that on a given Monday morning your desk will be overflowing with correspondence and documents for your urgent attention. There will be an administrative problem of some sort, which might involve finance, technology or personnel, or might have legal implications. And there will be a queue of people needing to see you. A lot of obstacles, in other words, to negotiate before you can begin to think strategically.

Apart from the day-to-day obstacles, there is a deep-seated resistance to change common to every organisation. This is the inertia that comes hard on the heels of achievement, the temptation to relax and enjoy the fruits of success that turns thrusting entrepreneurs into complacent bureaucrats. Temporary success can be the biggest single barrier to real achievement. We recognise it in every kind of organisation: governments that come to power on a wave of popular support and expectation but soon become accustomed to the trappings of power, and all too rapidly attract the indifference, even contempt, of the electorate; bars and restaurants that capture the popular *Zeitgeist* for a few heady months, only to close down within a year or two, unable to move with the times. The problem, it seems, is complacency.

That problem expresses itself in seven key areas, each of which you can influence for good or ill. These are the factors that make up an organisation, that can drive it forward or destroy it. They are the seven levers of change.

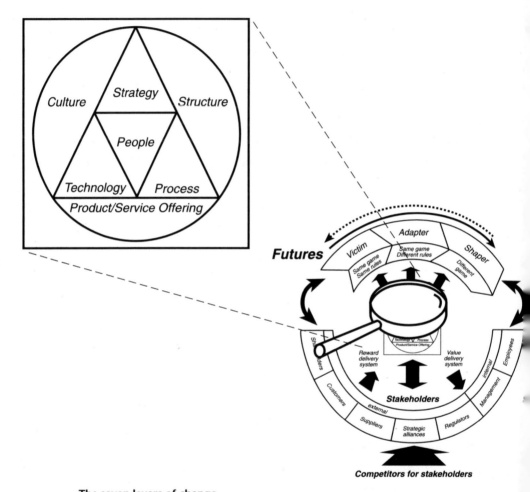

The seven levers of change

- To begin with, there's your current **strategy**, towards which your organisation will, presumably, be directed. If you have to change this, you have to change everything.

- Then there are your **people**. They have got used to working in a certain way, and they will not find it easy to make far-reaching changes; some may even have to go.
- The third problem is **process**; will you really have to re-engineer all your processes? Is it feasible?
- If you attempt such a move, you will certainly run into a fourth obstacle, which is your **structure**. Most organisations are to some extent departmentalised, and these departments may not be appropriate to a new customer-focused strategy. Restructuring is never easy.
- A fifth obstacle is your corporate **culture**. If your organisation has always presented itself and thought of itself in a certain way, can you now reinvent it? And can you be confident that staff and customers will both accept a new identity?
- The onward march of **technology** means that last year's revolutionary device for saving time and money can easily become next year's albatross. Radical change usually requires an element of new technology, and the ditching of some old. And that means retraining.
- Finally, there are the **products and services** themselves. Do you have the courage to jettison previously successful products or services because you believe they may be about to be overtaken?

As the chief executive ticks off each of these formidable seven obstacles, he may be tempted to conclude that it just isn't worth it. Why jeopardise the whole organisation for the sake of a new strategy that may not work? Why not carry on as we are, as long as we are trading profitably? Because that way your victim status is assured. If you don't have a vision and the courage to pursue it, your days are numbered. Besides, it is entirely up to you whether you identify these seven items as obstacles or levers of change. Let's just run through them again, with a positive twist this time:

- For all the reasons discussed in the last two chapters, we've decided to go against the flow and adopt a new **strategy**.
- To that end, the first thing we're going to do is involve our **people**. In fact, they will almost certainly help us to formulate that strategy.
- We'll make sure that our **processes** enable people to work more effectively . . .
- and that our **structure** is flexible enough so that people know what their roles are but have the freedom to use their imagination.
- Our **culture** is changing already, because we've involved everyone and begun to think about our organisation in a new way. All of a sudden, there are many more possibilities out there.
- **Technology** may give us new options. For instance, if we can offer our customers e-commerce opportunities, we might be able to cut costs and expand our markets simultaneously.
- At the end of it all, we might find ourselves with substantially different **products and services**. But, if that's what our customers want, that's what we're here for. So let's make a start.

You get the idea, I'm sure. And it's significant that as soon as you start to think in the right way it becomes obvious that you can't address one of the seven levers without addressing the others more or less simultaneously. They interact in so many ways as to be inseparable. And yet the extraordinary thing is how often people try to tackle one or two in isolation – and come unstuck in the process. Managing change must be a holistic process or it will not work.

Strategy – make the future your own

Successful strategy means not only being prepared to break with past practice but using your imagination to make the future your own. Classical strategy, as we have already discussed, contains an intrinsic assumption that there is a future out there, some kind of extension from the past and present, shaped by forces beyond our control. The aim, if you stick to classical strategy, is to analyse past and current trends, competitive behaviour and other known factors, in order to arrive at the best possible guess about the future. Identify threats and opportunities, and decide accordingly how to act.

There are certain circumstances in which classical strategy can still be effective. Developing countries, or those with autocratic or authoritarian regimes, often lack the democratic checks and balances to allow free markets to work; in many of these you would simply be asking for trouble if you were to seek to create discontinuities. There are also a handful of industries where there are effective monopolies or duopolies, and it is not in the interests of you or your competitor to attempt to change the rules of the game. Civil aircraft manufacture is an example, with Airbus and Boeing the only two manufacturers of global significance, and neither would wish to allow the entry of a third competitor. In all but these exceptional circumstances, we reject classical strategy.

In going against the flow, we believe that there are a number of futures out there, and you should aim to choose the one that suits you best. Ideally you will create your own discontinuity so that you are not at the mercy of someone else's. But it may work just as well if you choose a future that allows you to change the rules of the game in order to make the competition irrelevant. Whether that requires new products and services will depend on your customers; whether it requires new processes will depend largely on your people; whether you need new technology or a new organisational structure, or a combination of all these changes, will depend on the nature of the challenge you face.

This type of aspirational strategy depends above all upon your fitness for purpose. The right strategy, after all, is useless without the means to execute it. Consider a great strategist – Napoleon. Until megalomania got the better of him after the return from Elba, he outwitted his opponents almost entirely by superior strategy. Always securing his lines of supply, he ensured that his army could travel light, and he never fought battles on territory of his opponents' choosing.

But Napoleon realised that success depended on more than having the best ideas, the best battle plans. It required an army capable of executing those plans more quickly and effectively than the enemy. It required preparation, training, motivation and discipline. The whole organisation must be aligned with the strategy in order for it to work.

Business is not so different. Imaginative ideas and bold ambitions are useless unless your organisation is fit for its chosen purpose. Having chosen a strategy, you must align the other prime levers of change. This

The frustration gap

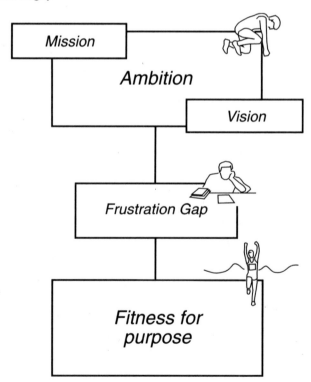

is never easy, and the gap between ambition and fitness for purpose is what I call the frustration gap. You know what you want to achieve, if only you could align every other part of your organisation with your vision. That frustration gap appears at many points, and we shall look at various ways of bridging it.

People – capability, motivation and opportunity

Let's take people first. There are three facets to making your people fit to execute your purpose. The first is capability, which is a combination of inherent capacity, intellectual or physical, to do the job; skills, which are acquired through coaching and on-the-job learning; and knowledge, which is about education and assimilation. The second facet is motivation. Once you have decided on a new direction, you need to consider how to change your people's behaviour and habits; that will require new measures, probably a new reward structure. Finally, people need opportunity. That means deploying the right people for the right jobs: for instance, those who are good at interpersonal skills might be put in customer-facing roles; those with greater analytical skills might be deployed in the back office. And, of course, if you recognise a person's unique qualities and put them in a role ideally suited to them, you will enormously improve their motivation – without having to pay them more! There's no substitute for taking this kind of trouble with your staff. They are, after all, one of your most powerful levers of change.

Many customer relationships depend crucially on the person at the counter, the receptionist, the salesperson or whoever happens to be the first line of contact. The bigger the organisation, the greater the danger of what I call the civil-service mentality – that the customer is essentially a nuisance. This may sound like a generalised slur on civil servants, but the fact is that civil servants are not usually directly answerable to the public. Their role is to execute the will of government. You may argue that they are only executing the will of the people as expressed through their elected representatives, and must ultimately be publicly accountable; the reality, however, is that they worry primarily about their internal reporting. The pubic, the end-customer in this case, can only hamper them in the carrying out of their duties. So make sure that your staff who deal with customers have the necessary personal qualities.

Often this is a matter of personality – 'extroverts front office, introverts back office' is a crude but often workable guide. But training can also make a huge difference.

Think of the US department of immigration. Think of parking wardens. Think of bailiffs. Or think of the employees of large companies and institutions – because the larger an organisation the more limited the responsibilities of the people within it, and the greater their regimentation and inflexibility. Nationalised industries are traditionally the worst, which is hardly surprising, since employees of the state cannot be expected to feel the commercial imperative as keenly as those who have always known that their jobs depend on satisfying customers. Newly privatised companies are perhaps the most fascinating studies in exploiting human resources – the important lesson being that your people, your employees, are your biggest asset or your biggest liability, depending almost entirely on your ability to motivate them.

Customer reaction will tell you a lot. British Airways, such a conspicuous success when privatisation led to a complete change of attitude among the staff in the early 1980s, fell back gradually in public esteem through the 1990s. Specific failings are hard to pinpoint. It was just that customers no longer felt they mattered in the way they once had. Many of the same staff who had delighted their customers five or ten years earlier seemed to have lost their touch. Why? Clearly not because they were unsuitable or incompetent. It could only be a failure of motivation.

Talking to staff, training and retraining them, is not enough. Human nature is such that the good intentions of today can easily be forgotten tomorrow – unless incentives are built in. The challenge for every organisation that wants to get the best out of its people is to create a reward system that links behaviour to results. Anglogold, the world's largest gold-mining company, provides a good case study.

When Bobby Godsell took over as chief executive after South Africa's conversion to democratic majority rule in 1994, motivation was his prime concern. The fall of the gold price and the emergence of militancy among the miners in the 1980s exposed the old system of white bosses ordering around thousands of ill-educated black workers as not merely unjust and unsustainable, but inefficient. As Godsell explained in an interview with the *Financial Times* in July 1998, 'Because of very high margins, the South African gold industry had become more of an engineering project than a business. It was about moving ground, it was about producing gold, consuming electricity and employing people.' Managers knew how much rock they had moved and how much gold they had produced, but they had no idea about profits or dividends. Godsell began by setting a new strategic aim. He told his people: 'Guys, we don't care if we're the biggest gold miner in the world. We want to be the most profitable.' To align his staff with this objective, he introduced a system of bonuses, to cover everyone from chief executive to face worker; the aim was to make bonuses constitute at least a third of everyone's total pay. A share incentive scheme for executives has to wait for a change in South Africa's tax laws, but it is a remarkable tribute to Godsell's personnel-management skills that he managed to avoid serious labour unrest while cutting the workforce by nearly half over five years. Anglogold was listed in June 1998 in Johannesburg, London, Brussels and Paris, and its share price rose swiftly in the ensuing months.

There are limits to payment by results. For a while in the 1980s, banks all over the world paid their traders handsomely in line with the massive profits they made for their employers. If they had not done so, they knew that their best traders would have been snapped up by competitors. The result was that an elite of traders made bigger and bigger profits, raising the stakes every time, so that, wittingly or unwittingly, they began to take bigger and bigger risks – until 1995, when, in quick succession, three rogue traders were exposed with cataclysmic consequences for their employers. At Daiwa Bank, Toshihide Iguchi ran up losses of £700 million, playing the US treasury markets. He was outdone by the Singapore trader Nick Leeson, who lost £830 million, bringing down Barings Bank in the process. In 1996 Yasuo Hamanaka confessed to ten years of unauthorised trading, totalling losses of £1.2 billion for his employer, the Japanese commodities and industrial giant Sumitomo.

The dilemma for financial institutions was, and is: how to continue motivating traders to look for better results but at the same time reduce the company's exposure? The answer is to link exposure to results so that you can measure risk-adjusted results. It isn't easy but it can be done, and, when traders who gamble and win discover that their reward is not as great as they had anticipated, they will soon moderate their behaviour. The challenge, of course, is to create a mechanism that is ideally balanced. Without risk, there can be no reward, for company and trader alike, so it is vital that risk taking per se be not penalised. The penalty must kick in only when the company is excessively exposed – and those targets and limits may vary from week to week. For everyone's benefit, therefore, this is another issue on which the employee must be consulted at every stage.

If people have a financial stake in the company, they are that much more likely to equate the company's success with their own. Microsoft is just one of many keen advocates of the employee-shareholder, and the idea is far from new. The John Lewis Partnership, a British retail chain founded between the wars by a socialist entrepreneur, has always operated on a democratic, almost communist model in which every employee is a shareholder, and decisions are taken by works councils.

Holding to the slogan 'Never knowingly undersold', JLP has prospered steadily for more than fifty years. It may not have set the high street alight with innovation, but, where other retail chains have sparked and fizzled for a while before dying out, JLP has made the unfailing helpfulness and commitment of its staff the key to its longevity.

Another way of ensuring the lasting commitment of your staff – and of retaining them – is by constantly striving to increase their market value. Forget the negative idea that you might train someone to a certain level, only for another employer to poach them and reap the benefit of your investment. In the long run, the employer who provides the most opportunities for career development and job satisfaction will attract and retain the best people. We shall develop this theme in the next chapter, as we consider employees as stakeholders.

Process – building in efficiency, quality and effectiveness

Processes have three roles, all crucial in ensuring your organisation's fitness for purpose. First, they should build in efficiency, ensuring that a certain input results in the maximum possible output – and that that process can be repeated at will. This kind of reliability makes cost control very much easier. Secondly, they should ensure quality control: they are designed to eliminate rogue behaviour, and experience will prove whether they can do this; once tested, such processes provide a safety net, insurance against human error. Finally, processes should guarantee effectiveness by codifying best practice for delivering the strategy of the organisation. This is vitally different from efficiency: a process may be efficient, but internally focused. To be effective, a process must be closely aligned with customer needs.

In small organisations, lack of process can be a barrier to development. Every time someone wants to do something new, they have to create a process from scratch – often a punitively time-consuming task. There is a risk that people will do things wrong. Without processes, people may attempt to pursue their own initiatives regardless of others. Having created their own processes, they will claim ownership of them, and, before you know where you are, you will have created an organisation of prima donnas.

The problems for large organisations are quite different. Whereas small businesses, often directed by a single individual, should have no difficulty in retaining customer focus, large companies take a lot more running. One person can't do it all, so specific functions are delegated, and systems are instituted to ensure that no area of business is neglected. The tendency is for people to be organised in functional silos, following particular lines of reporting, becoming more and more isolated from the end-customer.

Derek Wanless, chief executive of National Westminster Bank, acknowledged as much when he told his top 200 managers in April 1998: 'If we cling to our hierarchical, process-driven structure, we will not survive.' NatWest, like many other large financial institutions, was a prime example in 1998 of the system-driven organisation. Its systems had been designed to achieve product focus while reducing costs, not to encourage customer-service enhancements. Its branch structure was organised for internal administrative purposes, not for the customer's benefit.

We are back with the civil-service mentality – common enough in banks, where typically one department will deal with day-to-day deposits and withdrawals, another with loans, another with foreign currency, and perhaps others with insurance or ancillary financial services. So if a customer were to find work abroad and wish to make various alterations to his or her banking arrangements – retaining one account but closing another, altering the details of insurance policies, and perhaps creating new accounts to deal with regular payments to dependent children, finance companies, or whatever – the chances are they would have to make several different arrangements with different departments. Why? The customer is dealing with only one bank, and would certainly like to deal with all these details via a single interview, or a single written instruction. But the bank that will take care of all such matters for you remains the exception rather than the rule. Why? Because the processes and structures have been designed for the bank's benefit, not the customer's.

The same is true of many hospitals, where procedures have been developed at the instigation and for the convenience of doctors, nurses and hospital staff, with patients coming a poor fourth. In Britain's National Health hospitals, it remains commonplace for doctors or nurses to brush aside a patient's enquiry or request on the grounds that 'I'm just coming to the end of my shift' – an instinctive reaction that says everything about the patient/customer's place in the pecking order.

None of this means that processes should be regarded as negative factors within an organisation. On the contrary, they represent a codified approach to doing business that is essential if standards are to be built in. Without this kind of codification, an organisation cannot change, lead change, or even effectively react to changes in the market-place since it cannot possibly know what it knows; even worse, it will be ignorant about its own areas of ignorance. Utterly lacking in self-awareness, such a company will be able to do only one thing: imitate its competitors. Alternatively, it will be able to acquire knowledge only by acquiring another company. Create properly codified practices, however, and you are well on the way to creating the true learning organisation in which individual knowledge and expertise is harnessed so that it can be shared and applied throughout the company.

Let me give you an example. Four years ago, a global food manufac-turer decided to embark on partnerships with its suppliers to rationalise processes and thereby reduce the total cost of purchasing. When you consider that in this industry purchasing costs account for about 60 per cent of the cost of food, rationalisation sounds both elementary and essential. Yet, when this programme was begun, it was discovered that there was no company-wide process: it all depended which subsidiary was buying which goods from which supplier. On the major cost-driving issue of the moment, there was no codification, with the result that the company's financial director was effectively working in the dark! This was a company that was contemplating a major effort to alter the rules of the game: a radical rebranding exercise in the face of widespread media suggestions that the success of supermarkets' own-label branding was making the very concept of brand value redundant. As a part of the new process codification, the company brought its suppliers' engineers and managers together with its own engineers, managers, buyers and marketing personnel at the product-design stage: the suppliers made their latest technology available, enabling new savings that the company could not have achieved merely by rationalising its sources of supply. Without this significant reduction in purchasing costs, the company's rebranding exercise might well have fallen flat.

Codified business processes (CBPs) of this kind can be a vital tool for capturing and disseminating organisational learning, in four main ways. First, CBPs become the formal model for doing business in a particular area, where it represents collective organisational wisdom. Secondly, every time we learn ways of doing the job better, we update the CBPs and amend our files and training programmes accordingly. Thirdly, we define measurements by which we can monitor the CBPs' effectiveness, and take remedial action when necessary. Finally, when we decide to go against the flow, we identify those CBPs that need changing, while leaving intact those that can continue to work as before. Without CBPs, major-change programmes will almost invariably involve changing a number of processes that don't really need changing; in large organisations, such waste of effort and resources can be crippling.

We shall return to the subject of knowledge management in Chapter 6.

Structure – and why it can only disable

In large organisations, speed of execution and an ability to create discontinuities are almost chimerical aspirations. I have had chief executives come to me and ask how they can transform their organisation to align it behind a new strategy. Their frustration is painful to see – the task is so intimidating. Of course it is. You might as well try to persuade a Rolls-Royce to manoeuvre like a jeep, or make an ocean liner perform like a speedboat. With large organisations, you need to tackle the frustration gap in a different way. There is simply no chance of transforming a large international airline, a bank with half a million employees, or an industrial giant with factories round the world so that it can support an ideal of flexibility and responsiveness. Know your limitations. In cases like these, the answer is not to concentrate on the fitness for purpose until you have first reduced the scale of your ambition. This is the other way of narrowing the frustration gap.

The challenge is not to become obsessed with the 80 per cent of the company that is intractable, but to identify the 20 per cent where changes can be made. You have to identify the points of articulation – where there is flexibility in the mechanism – and work on those. If you can find the compelling link that will enable your Rolls-Royce or ocean liner to turn, you can be sure that the rest of the organisation will follow.

Whereas your people are potentially your biggest asset, structures can only disable. In the first place, they tend to turn people's attention inwards. By creating silos, they automatically create barriers between people working in different silos. And, when head office becomes too powerful, demanding or controlling, other parts of the organisation feel left out, resentments built up, and the conduit between the strategic head and the arm that reaches out to the customer becomes ineffective. In her book *The Change Masters*, Rosabeth Moss Kanter contrasts the experiences of ITT and GE Medical Systems. At ITT, an elite corps of financial managers meant that finance became the investigator, policeman, judge and jury in all crucial decision making. The financial managers planted within each division had a stronger allegiance to the head of corporate finance than to the divisional heads to whom they were supposed to report. As a result, a short-term bottom-line-oriented culture prevailed, gradually destroying the competitive edge of each of the divisions that had enabled the company to penetrate its various markets. We shall return to this theme in Chapter 8.

Moss Kanter contrasts the ITT experience with that of GE Medical Systems, where managers reported both to the function where the manager worked and to a connected office where tasks were integrated for particular products. Although the dotted-line relationship was often ill-defined, it helped the manager by providing access to another powerful superior capable of offering support, resources and information. It also meant managers could cross formal lines without feeling they were violating protocol.

The most successful companies are not exactly unstructured. They are the ones whose structure provides the fewest barriers to the implementation of a new strategy. Think again of Richard Branson and Virgin. This is an organisation where Branson himself may fly the plane or serve the drinks, and where a pilot or stewardess may come up with the bright idea that will be pursued as company policy. Equally crucially, whenever Branson has a new idea, he simply sets up a new company, so that he is not disabled by his existing structure.

Structures, however logical, inevitably become barriers. And yet an organisation, by definition, requires organising. The challenge is to organise it in such a way that the structure disables as little as possible.

At St Luke's, the London advertising agency, where every employee acquires a share in the company as soon as they have completed a six-month apprenticeship, the corporate structure can never be rigid because every year the shareholder/owners vote in a new board of six trustees to run the company. The St Luke's vision is 'To Open Minds', and Andy Law, the company's founder and chairman, has always stressed the need to keep exploring. As he explains it in his book *Open Minds*, 'St Luke's changes each year, because its owners change. These owners come into St Luke's on an understanding that we keep exploring. If we ever stop exploring, we will be as guilty as everyone else of finding a formula and blindly sticking to it.'

As St Luke's became more successful and hired more people, Andy Law became worried about the small-company ethos and dynamism disappearing. His answer was what he called the 'Citizen Cell Structure', based on the notion that thirty-five people is 'about as big as you can get before you cease to care about the people with whom you directly work'. St Luke's consists, therefore, of several self-managed groups, each run by an operational head with complete authority over its modus operandi, budgets and income streams. A spirit of friendly rivalry prevails between the cells, which are bonded to the whole by the share scheme, departmental and personal affinities, and a need to share certain resources such as IT, marketing, catering and cleaning. Whenever a group exceeds thirty-five, it must split and form two groups. By this 'Amoeba Growth System', Law hopes that St Luke's will retain the passion and collaborative spirit of the small company, as well as a capacity for 'instant, unprogrammed fun'.

For the rest of us, there simply is no ideal organisational structure. Depending on what you want to achieve, you may wish to change your structure, not to enable anything, but simply in order to avoid disabling your new strategic intent. So how do you measure the extent to which your current structure is disabling you? Map the new processes you have just introduced, and see how many interfaces, or links, are created. If the chain of command is long, the potential for disablement is that much greater. Can you reduce the number of interfaces – both personal and technical? If you can, then you should probably make a structural adjustment.

Of course, as soon as you make structural adjustments, you have to make sure that your internal processes are compatible; above all, you need to check your financial control mechanisms. If you continue to apply the old financial measurement systems to new structures, you are liable to create new areas of conflict that will hamper implementation of any new strategy.

Culture – identity, rituals, stories and symbols

Moving on from the specifics of process and structure, we come to the whole corporate culture – this pervasive feeling that an organisation stands for something, that we've always done things in a certain way and that, if we were to abandon our tried and trusted methods, we would lose our identity.

So much depends on definition. Theodore Levitt traces the demise of US Railways back to the fact that the company, having opened up the American continent so spectacularly, setting the world an example for innovation in passenger transport, refused to think of itself as being in anything other than the railway business. As a result, it had no answer when the motor car and the aeroplane became the favoured mode of transport. Had it simply redefined itself as the American Transport Company, it might have gone into partnership with Ford or Boeing, or at least made an effort to provide effective links with airports and major road networks. And the United States might still have a rail network worthy of the name.

As Gerry Johnson has pointed out in his book *Exploring Corporate Strategy*, a cultural system, in which the various parts of an organisation all work towards a common end, can be a source of strength. Conversely, it can easily be a source of weakness by making it very difficult to change. Johnson has developed what he calls the 'cultural web', in which the core is the general perception of an organisation (what he calls the 'paradigm', but which I prefer in this context to call image). This core is surrounded by six overlapping elements, of which three are organisational and three personal. I am concerned here only with the personal ones which reflect the way people in an organisation think about themselves, and the underlying assumptions they make in their day-to-day conversations. He has composed a revealing study of Britain's National Health Service by investigating these six elements and their effect on the organisation's image, or paradigm.

The first of the three personal elements is ritual or routine – the daily habits that make up 'the way we do things around here', the formal processes such as training programmes, assessment procedures or sales conferences, and the informal processes such as chatting by the photocopier or drinking in the local bar after work. In the NHS, these rituals and routines – consultations, prescription of drugs, bedtimes and mealtimes for patients – reinforce the perception that doctors and nurses know best. They become a handicap when they make staff unreceptive to enquiries or complaints from patients. If the NHS really means what it says about patient care, it could certainly look at some of these routines, and consider ways in which patients could be given more choice, empowered to make more decisions on their own behalf.

The second element is stories – the tales people tell about successes, disasters, heroes and villains. These can be enormously revealing. In the NHS, the heroes are nearly always the staff, and the villains politicians and administrators. All very well, but hardly conducive to a constructive attitude from staff to any administrative changes. Other organisations have similar problems. In my own firm, KPMG, the stories have tended to be about individuals pulling off brilliant deals. There has been a macho element that has its downside: when you are trying to encourage a collegiate approach in which information is shared and minds are kept open, the last thing you want is people who think they can do it all on their own, and set their course with single-minded purpose, oblivious to the opinions of colleagues.

One chief executive, determined to circulate new kinds of stories round his office, would occasionally dictate a memo to his secretary, then ask her to mark it 'highly confidential' and leave a copy on the photocopier as if by mistake. He was gratified to discover that these stories rapidly became common currency and contributed to a gradual culture change.

Then there are the symbols. These can take many different forms, but in almost every organisation of a certain size, there are umpteen symbols that differentiate one member of staff from another: titles, dress, cars, size of office, privileges and nuances of language. In the NHS, there are obvious differences in uniform. In our own offices, there used to be many subtle symbols differentiating people according to seniority – the most obvious being size of office. One of my first initiatives when I took over KPMG's Business Transformation Unit was to ensure that, as far as possible, everyone had offices of a similar size. Bill Gates has done the same at Microsoft: it means that, when strategies, priorities or dispositions change, people can move from one more or less identical office to another – there is no culture shock.

Gates did not want a conventional organisation, organised into departments, with layers of executive authority. He believed that to develop software what people needed more than anything else was somewhere to 'sit and think', away from the hustle and bustle, out of the mainstream. Offices were designed to be functional, and private. Since they were more or less identical throughout the campus, there was no pecking order; and, as the organisation changed, offices could be swapped any time, without fuss – nothing to distract anyone from sitting and thinking.

IBM, by contrast, displayed the scolding message 'THINK!' on its walls, while expecting people to perform this vital task in what Randall Stross describes as 'open-space bullpens'. Over at Wang Laboratories in Massachusetts, the chairman, An Wang, had his office at the top of one of the towers that dominated Wang's central facility. Access to the chairman was severely restricted, and the vertical design gave all who entered a physical sense of the hierarchy within. The power of symbols is obvious as soon as we give them some thought. Why else would we pay design companies such huge sums to come up with appropriate logos? And yet people in business constantly allow symbols to dominate in ways that are thoroughly detrimental to their organisations.

Technology – make sure it doesn't restrict your vision

A lack of technology can be an enormous barrier to change, as can the wrong type of technology. Every substantial business today is dependent, to a great extent, on systems management. But the legacy systems that were created to describe the environment of yesterday, or even today, may be a liability tomorrow. Japanese motor manufacturers, for instance, invested heavily in new technology in the 1970s and 1980s, when the rest of the world gasped in awe at their use of robots, and automated production lines; but by the 1990s much of this technology was out of date, and the Japanese were overtaken by US car makers with simplified assembly processes.

Similarly, banks that designed systems to capture customer information have since found themselves unable to compete with masters of technology like Capital One.

As Thomas Davenport explained in an article in the *Harvard Business Review* in July 1998, 'if you're not careful, the dream of information integration can turn into a nightmare.' Davenport cites the examples of Foxmeyer Drug, which went into bankruptcy blaming its computer system; Mobil Europe, which spent hundreds of millions of dollars on new systems only to merge with BP and find that the new systems were surplus to requirements; and Dell, which found that its system clashed with its new, decentralised management model.

Technology that is too specific can prove suddenly irrelevant when the game moves on. Organisations can often make the mistake of wanting to have their own bespoke technology, computer systems that take account of their own unique features. What then if the organisation has to reinvent itself?

Technology can be a barrier in other ways: by being limited to measuring operational matters; by being capable only of dealing with past or present factors; by creating information overload so that people spend too much time analysing or processing superfluous data; or, worst of all, by creating a system that people don't trust – so that they create their own systems, and the organisation loses coherence and discipline.

On the other hand, new systems can produce dramatic improvements in productivity and speed. Autodesk, a leading maker of computer-aided-design software, used to take an average of two weeks to deliver an order to a customer. Now, having installed an Enterprise System (ES), it ships 98 per cent of its orders within twenty-four hours. IBM's Storage Systems division reduced the time required to reprice all of its products from five days to five minutes, the time to ship a replacement part from twenty-two days to three days, and the time to complete a credit check from twenty minutes to three seconds.

The danger of an ES package is when a single one is used by virtually every company in an industry. Such convergence around a single software package should raise a sobering question in the minds of chief executives: how similar can our information flows and our processes be to those of our competitors before we begin to undermine our own sources of differentiation in the market?

This doesn't apply to a company like Apple, whose unique operating system and strong brand differ dramatically from competing offerings. But most other companies rely on differentiation based on service and price rather than on product. For those companies, there is a very real risk that an enterprise system could dissolve their sources of advantage.

The trouble with many of the most powerful and effective systems is that they impose their own logic on organisations that should be following a different set of priorities. Compaq was aware of this danger, and decided that, although a fully integrated enterprise system was essential, it would invest in writing its own proprietary applications to support its forecasting and order-management processes. Compaq saw the decision as a strategic necessity: it was the only way to protect a potentially critical source of advantage.

Air Products and Chemicals is another company that saw its competitors installing large ES programs, but decided not to follow their lead. After a thorough evaluation, APC weighed up the cost of having to raise its prices in the commodity gas markets in order to pay for the systems, and decided that while existing systems were not state-of-the-art, they were adequate. And, since the company had no plans to exchange information electronically with competitors, it didn't worry about going against the flow and being the odd man out in its industry.

Of the fifty or so ES-dependent companies studied by Davenport, the ones found to be the most successful were those that used it with a contrarian strategy. Whereas most companies stress the word 'system' and not the word 'enterprise', Elf Atochem North America, a $2 billion regional chemicals subsidiary of the French company Elf Aquitaine, is the opposite. After a series of mergers the company felt an enterprise system would be the best way to integrate the data flows. Crucially, however, they never labelled the ES project as simply a technology initiative. Instead, the company saw it as a chance to take a fresh look at its strategy and organisation. By looking beyond the technology, the executives came to realise that the real source of Elf Atochem's difficulties was not the diversity of its systems but the fragmentation of its entire organisation.

Elf Atochem also made a special effort to maintain its focus on the customer and decided to install a program in just four key processes: materials management, production planning, order management and financial reporting. The most important step was to use the system to gather real-time information needed to connect sales and production planning – demand and supply – for the first time. As orders are entered or changed, the system automatically updates forecasts and factory schedules, thus enabling the company to alter its production runs almost instantly, in response to customers' needs. Even though many competitors were also adopting SAP's R/3 package, only one other company had developed this capability, which meant that Elf Atochem gained an important edge.

In Chapter 9 we shall examine the management of technology in greater depth, but the extranet is a development worth mentioning here. Whereas intranets are systems for knowledge management and administrative convenience within companies, extranets fulfil the same function for affinity groups – making it possible that entire business cultures may be changing for ever. Already, solicitors are able to search extranets to find out from estate agents when houses come up for sale, so they can offer their services. Announcements in newspapers, for many decades a prime source of new business leads for traders, are coming to seem out of date. If you can get hold of the same information twenty-four hours earlier, you have a crucial competitive advantage. Suddenly the game could be changing: where once the advantage belonged to those with the best personal contacts, it may soon belong to those with greater speed of access to information about potential new markets.

Of course technology will never take over from personal contact, but in certain contexts it offers unanswerable advantages. Only a fool ignores the scope of such new technology.

Products and services – bridging the customer's frustration gap

When it comes to products and services, the requirements for success seem relatively straightforward. Quality, reliability and all the other desirable properties are secondary to the overriding requirement, which is customer satisfaction. Providers will usually wish to ensure that their product is in some way unique – for if it can be replicated it becomes no more than a commodity, subject to price pressure. At the very least, therefore, we strive to add some element of service or expertise that ensures that the customer will come to us rather than our rivals. Confronted with a choice between several shops selling the same goods at similar prices, shoppers are likely to opt for the shop whose staff are most helpful and expert. Other considerations, like marketing and distribution, are equally vital. The best products in the world will never sell if people don't know about them, or if they cannot receive them on time.

But there must also be a willingness to change the product utterly if the market requires it. We have seen how IBM famously failed to do this. By contrast, observers of the car industry like Richard Pascale were struck by the way Honda, the Japanese manufacturer, was flexible enough in the late 1980s to develop a radically different engine, the CVCC, as a rapid and outstandingly successful response to US pollution controls. But it was more than this that led Richard Pascale to claim in *Managing on the Edge* that Honda was 'arguably the best managed company in the world'.

Honda recognised that willingness to change the product was just one feature of the organisational mindset required. The 'Honda Way' relied upon the careful selection, training and rewarding of employees in line with its priorities in research, engineering and manufacturing.

The frustration gap, which I introduced earlier in this chapter, is a useful model for looking at products and services. The temptation is always for an organisation to think of itself in terms of its products and services. Many, indeed, are more or less defined by their products: we think of Coca-Cola as a drink, Rolls-Royce as a motor car, Versace as clothes, and so on. But really these are companies that manufacture something that bridges the frustration gap for their customers. You may recall that in my model the gap comes between ambition and fitness for purpose. From the customer's point of view, their ambition, or need, may be refreshment, or speed, or something more nebulous like style.

In the case of Versace, Dior or Ralph Lauren, it is perhaps easier to see that the customer is not buying clothes so much as an image. The product itself doesn't matter as much as what it represents. Fashion designers, in fact, are prime examples of running businesses against the flow. One has only to think of Liz Hurley and 'that dress', the low-cut black Versace gown slashed down the side and held together with giant safety-pins that was the most photographed dress of the 1990s, to be reminded of fashion's essential shock value. Once designers become conventional or predictable, they may continue to produce goods of a certain quality or style, but their marketability is in decline.

The ever-present danger is complacency. Honda's solution was to break the company apart in a far more radical fashion than had ever occurred before in the motor industry, into three separate companies: R&D, Engineering and the Honda Motor Company. The thinking, as Pascale puts it, was that the tension between these three companies 'each highly independent, yet each interdependent, was the best way of arresting decay'. The next requirement is for the creative tension to be allowed to simmer. This is done by holding sessions in which subordinates can openly question bosses and challenge the status quo. Pascale points to how this 'sustains a restless, self-questioning atmosphere that one expects to see in new ventures – yet Honda is into its fourth generation of management. Its founders retired in 1970.'

More specifically, there is also the problem of investment – investment of money, time, people, effort, imagination, commitment and all kinds of other resources, physical and intellectual. We all invest – in clothes, for instance. And, when we are required to make a radical change, it is not unlike being asked to part with an entire wardrobe – not just the favourite suits (probably the costliest items) but also the shirts or scarves chosen by spouses, even the lovingly darned or patched socks or sweaters. And sometimes the investment, whether financial or emotional or both, is too large.

A contemporary example on a very different scale springs to mind. For a number of global organisations, particularly in financial services, there is a technological-investment dilemma that promises to endure for a few years yet: smart card or magnetic-strip card? The question is easy to answer if you have made no investment. Smart-card technology – in which a tiny computer chip is embedded in a plastic card – is so much more versatile that it should be no contest. For consumers, smart cards can be programmed to perform every vital task, from banking to shopping, from booking tickets to opening the garage door. A smart card can contain your medical records, blood group and DNA identity, while simultaneously enabling you to withdraw money anywhere in the world, or make any number of commercial transactions. For companies, their possibilities are almost limitless. And for governments they promise any number of improvements in security and monitoring.

Yet the magnetic-strip card endures. It too is versatile and easy to use –

just not so versatile as the smart card. More to the point, cash machines and tills all over the world are programmed to deal with magnetic-strip cards. The United States being the world leader in financial services, and having invested massively in magnetic-strip technology, the cash cards and debit cards that you may hold in your wallet are hardly likely to become redundant overnight. Nor, indeed, is the smart card's ultimate victory assured. As Betamax and Apple have shown, superior technology is not everything. And yet it does seem more than probable that the smart card's victory can only be postponed, for, once we can perform a certain number of essential tasks with a smart card – and realise that we should be able to perform every other vital task with that same card – will we accept the inconvenience of using so many separate cards?

Whichever way this particular contest is resolved, the moral is clear. A new market entrant will be at an advantage through having made no investment. If smart-card technology prevails, those who have invested in magnetic-strip technology will be burdened with an almost worthless legacy. And, if the stranglehold of magnetic-strip technology is not broken, all that investment in smart cards may yet come to nothing in commercial terms. Ten, twenty or thirty years hence, the chances are that the battle for supremacy in this market will be won not by one of the established banks or consortia but by a late entrant with no investment baggage who is best able to anticipate and satisfy the demands of the customer.

Excessive investment in technology, in particular products and services, and in people and structures, too, can be seen in retrospect as the key factor in IBM's decline in the 1980s. With new revenue records being set each year in the early part of that decade, it did not occur to the company's leaders to notice the clouds gathering on the horizon. The staff, taking their cue from above, carried on in their set routines. Gradually, the clouds moved overhead. The first hints of real difficulty came from IBM's most sophisticated customers – those firms demanding leading-edge information technology. They complained that IBM's newest computers did not do what they wanted them to do – but, rather than examine why this was happening, IBM management seemed content just to let those customers go. Soon the clouds grew darker. New machines in the mainstream product line were slipping in quality. Customers began reporting late deliveries of new IBM machines, which, once installed, failed to reach anticipated performance levels. IBM's once-unassailable reputation for service and support was being called into question.

But the crucial problem was that proposals for change were seen as inconveniences and threats. The mainframe-manufacturing division did not want to believe that market forces were rendering existing technology obsolete; machines based on this technology were still earning IBM the bulk of its profits.

The career, prestige and pay of every manager in the group were tied to this technology; they had all grown up on it and would have had to re-educate themselves or retire if it were changed. The sales force, too, hated the notion of such a change. Replace well-known, high-margin computers with completely different machines with lower margins? Inconceivable.

In retrospect we can see that what made IBM so successful was also the root cause of its sudden decline. The company made two commitments, closely related to each other: promising its customers high-quality technology and excellent service support; and promising its employees job security. But in the late 1980s and early 1990s both contracts were broken.

As D. Quinn Mills and G. Bruce Friesen tell the story in their book *Broken Promises*,

Customers grew angry at IBM's arrogance – its faulty equipment, late deliveries, and failure to keep up with emerging technology available from other vendors. The company was even castigated for failures in its service – something unthinkable in earlier decades . . . Long allowed by their managers to believe that employment security had little reference to performance, thousands of employees had grown lax, as top-performing IBMers complained bitterly in attitude surveys.

There is a paradox here. For investment is essential. Success may begin with a great idea; but that idea must attract investment in order to work. And yet every investment carries with it the potential for inertia, the seeds of its own ultimate destruction. As Pascale puts it in *Managing on the Edge*, the paradox is that 'successful organisations *must* build paradigms – and having done so, are inevitably imperilled by them'. 'Inquiry' is Pascale's answer to the problem of ossification or complacency. Honda advocates conflict – although not every company would be able to master Honda's way of harnessing conflict, and ensuring that it is constructive, not destructive. Above all, perhaps, it is a willingness to take stock, to step outside your current situation, and be prepared to reinvent yourself, to surprise your friends, neighbours and competitors, even to surprise yourself, that can enable you to turn apparent barriers into levers of change.

The world of entertainment provides an interesting example in the comedian Jerry Seinfeld who, in 1998, turned down the chance of earning $5 million per show for his own comedy series, *Seinfeld*, because, 'in my business, the only way to get as much money as I have is if you don't care about money and you care about comedy, then, somehow you end up with money'. When he realised he had what seemed like the perfect package, he became wary of complacency and of a dip in quality on the show. Instead he decided to return to his roots as a stand-up comic. Seinfeld has done exactly what Pascale would have companies do: as he puts it, establish a paradigm, then break it. Phase 1 saw him make a success out of stand-up comedy; then he built on that in Phase 2 to create his own television series; and then he broke his paradigm in Phase 3 by returning to his roots.

Pascale calls it breaking a paradigm, others call it creating a discontinuity. It certainly fits our chosen metaphor in this book, for it clearly involves escaping from the mainstream. Every time you feel the current pulling you in a certain direction, your reaction should be to resist. You should do things for your own reasons, not because everyone else is doing them. If you see an easy option, be suspicious. Never be afraid to go against the flow.

In a stimulating article in the *Harvard Business Review* in July 1998, Nigel Nicholson suggests that business is to a great extent a battle to resist normal human instincts – the survival instincts that encourage people to sell when stocks are rising and that mistakenly prompt them to gamble out of panic, when they can least afford to. Evolutionary psychology means that emotions can never fully be suppressed. But Nicholson believes that the winners will be those who can most effectively harness their rational capacity to defy that current in human behaviour.

When a company announces impending lay-offs, productivity miraculously improves. Everyone's doing the same thing: working extra hard. But, when it's announced that entire divisions are to close, people cease to act rationally, and lash out in a panic to survive. Strikes, protests, loss of temper – all guaranteed to make things worse. Those who stay calm and rational, who reject the herd instinct and adapt to behaving in a way that the modern-day world demands, are the ones who will survive. Don't get mad, get even.

Nicholson asks us to imagine a bell curve. At one end are the habitual risk-takers – a dynamic breed confident enough in their ability and knowledge to know that this approach will see them succeed more than they fail. At the other end are the people who never take risks. 'What's the point?' they say. They have such confidence in their chosen path that they never need to stray from it. Both these characters are strong contrarians who are constantly going against the flow. The greatest successes will be found among their number. They are born leaders. But most people fall right in the middle of the curve, avoiding loss when comfortable with life, and fighting furiously when survival requires them to do so.

Nicholson refers to the countless management books that extol the virtues of confidence. I share his scepticism about such books. What good is confidence if it is based on misunderstanding – as it so often is? Going against the flow does not mean ploughing on regardless. It means analysing your situation with great care, being aware of dangers, and relying on knowledge, training and reason. And reason tells us we are all human, and liable to be wrong.

Pascale writes of 'the inherent tendency of the human mind (and organisations) to perceive patterns' – patterns which, over time, form a mental infrastructure. Danger arises, he says, when 'our mental maps cease to fit the territory'. But it's not only our mental maps, not only our mental infrastructure that limits our versatility. Organisations, created by humans with these tendencies, develop physical structures and processes that are, in many cases, even harder to change.

Hence the paradoxes we have just discussed. But paradoxes are a question of language, not of objective reality. In this chapter we have confronted some of these obstacles, and tried to explain how, by recalibrating the corporate mindset – or, to put it more plainly, by opening our minds – we can turn obstacles into levers of change, and set our organisations to forge upstream to success.

CHAPTER 4 – DIGEST

A new kind of competition

Key message:

Why compete only for customers or shareholders? What about the other stakeholders? Businesses will succeed only if they can develop a winning value proposition for each stakeholder.

Why?

Because every stakeholder is both customer and supplier, with the capacity to nourish your business – or harm it if they are neglected.

What?

The challenge: to gain the loyalty of stakeholders.

- Customers
- Shareholders
- Employees
- Suppliers
- Strategic allies
- Business managers
- Regulators

So what?

So deal as openly as possible with every stakeholder. Prioritise, then explain.

CHAPTER 4

A new kind of competition

In the hustle and bustle of the business mainstream, the name of the game is to get to the client or customer first. Find out what they want, and see if you can give it to them. Refine your product, improve your service, make customer satisfaction your goal, and you have a good chance of beating the competition. In the early days, such a single-minded approach may stand you in good stead. But the bigger you grow, the more complicated life becomes. Shareholders must be satisfied too. Gradually, you discover that what is good for the customer may not be so good for the shareholder – and vice versa. But balancing these two interests may not be enough. Your perspective is still far too narrow.

Business on the threshold of the twenty-first century is a much broader kind of competition than ever before. Why should you compete only for customers and shareholders? What if a competitor can poach all your best people? What if your staff become disgruntled, for whatever reason? These things will soon permeate to customers, and ultimately to shareholders too. And what about your suppliers? If a rival offers them a better deal, you could suddenly be deprived of your lifeblood.

You have to think in terms of satisfying all the stakeholders in your business. This means, in every substantial company, at least four primary stakeholders: customers, shareholders, employees and suppliers. Then,

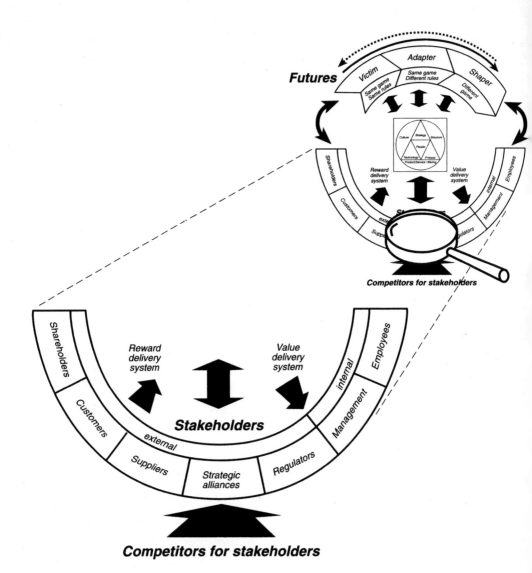

Competing for stakeholders

in larger companies, particularly those operating on a global scale, there are three ancillary stakeholders: business managers, strategic allies and regulators. Your task, which we shall explore in this chapter and the next, is to develop a value proposition for each.

First, it would be as well to understand what we mean by the term 'stakeholder'. For our purposes in this book, a stakeholder is an entity (person or organisation) with two distinct roles:

- A customer of value. The stakeholder's stake in your business implies that they seek from the business a certain value, i.e. a set of defined benefits that exceeds their cost of acquisition.
- A supplier of value. A shareholder, for instance, supplies value by buying shares at the offered price – enabling the business to raise money. But a business expects more: it looks to shareholders to show a degree of loyalty – company directors and management will hope that, at the least, they can persuade shareholders to trust them sufficiently not to sell their shares to the highest bidder at the first opportunity.

All stakeholders are both customers and suppliers. They are customers because they buy value from you. This is obvious in the case of the shareholder, who buys your shares and has certain expectations. It is less obvious, but equally true, in the case of employees, who work for you because this work earns them a measure of satisfaction, remuneration and prestige. It is even less obvious, but just as vital, in the case of regulators, who require certain things from you and may make your life difficult if they don't get them; from their point of view, the maintenance of health and safety or compliance with financial guidelines represents value. In each case, your job is to find out what represents value for the stakeholder, and offer the best you can – your value proposition.

At the same time, all these stakeholders are suppliers. Again, this is obvious with customers and shareholders who supply money, employees who supply work and suppliers who supply goods. But a regulator is just as surely a supplier – supplying you with permission to operate. Strategic allies fit easily into both categories, since allies are bound to have a relationship based on give and take.

To make life more difficult, there are any number of tensions between these stakeholders, these supplier/customers. At the most basic level, the more you reduce the price of a product for the customer's benefit the less you have to give your shareholder/employee. And the more you pay your employees the less money you have to spare to offer discounts to customers.

The one value that every business seeks from each stakeholder is loyalty. It is practically impossible for any organisation to deliver world-class value to all its stakeholders consistently over a long period. From time to time, there will be a dip in the delivery of that value, and that is when every organisation needs time to correct the situation. Loyalty is the value given by the stakeholder which buys the organisation time. Stakeholder loyalty is a generic value which deserves closer examination.

The twin-track approach to building customer loyalty

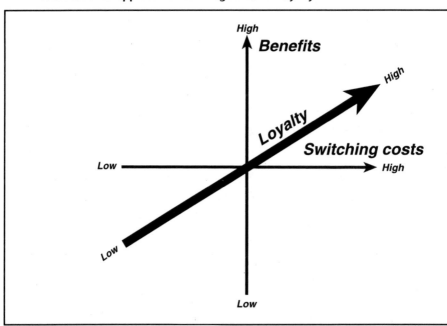

Customer Loyalty

From my experience with many different clients, I have identified two dimensions governing the concept of loyalty. On the positive side, the more value we offer the stakeholder, the more loyalty we can expect – limited, of course, by the value that the competition can offer. The value we can offer is inherent in our products and services, but however good these are (and however good the after-sales service and general reliability) this will not be enough to secure stakeholder loyalty. We need a negative dimension, too: something that will persuade the stakeholder that to leave would involve an undesirable amount of trouble, risk or pain. We need to make the switching costs as high as possible. For instance, the more we bundle our services to create a single solution to a client problem, the higher the costs for that client to switch to one of our competitors. Also, the more differentiated our product or service, the greater will be the switching cost.

The twin challenge, then, is to design value propositions for our stakeholders that include the dual concepts of intrinsic value and high switching costs.

It is a formidable challenge, and conventional responses are often defensive. Chief executives explain and justify themselves to business analysts, commentators and journalists in the hope that they will appreciate all the constraints, understand and endorse the basic strategy, and convey a favourable impression to shareholders and the wider public. But why be swept along by the business and media current in this way? You have no control over what people write, no guarantee that people will see things from your point of view, no way of preventing other people from bringing their own prejudices to bear.

Similarly, harassed executives worried about profit margins will treat an annual wage claim from a group of employees as one more obstacle to be circumvented as cheaply as possible. In this way, as we noted in the last chapter, one of the seven potential levers of change is treated as a barrier – and consequently becomes one. If you want to retain and motivate your staff, palming them off every year with the bare minimum is hardly the answer. And the macho assertion of management's 'right to manage' is no substitute for sensitive and sensible communication aimed at uncovering areas of mutual benefit. If you treat trade unions as enemies, that is exactly what they will become. The same goes for all the other stakeholders in your business.

Your task is to develop a value proposition for every stakeholder, and if you shirk that task you will fall into the reactive mindset that lies behind the short-termism that has bedevilled business, particularly in the US and the UK, and made corporate governance such an issue since 1990. When chief executives and company directors are so intellectually lazy, so easily pulled this way and that by the prevailing current, no wonder shareholders are keen to see independent non-executives on the board.

Let's examine the stakeholders in turn, and consider the value propositions we need to develop for each one.

1 Customers

A value proposition for the customer is a familiar concept. But how well is it understood? A century ago, value, whether in goods or services, was largely a matter of quality. Mass production techniques subsequently introduced the element of price competitiveness. Over the past two decades, computer technology has created new possibilities, and spurred competition for greater technical sophistication – latest-gizmo syndrome, we might call it. Now a kind of gizmo fatigue has set in, and people need to be convinced that technology is genuinely useful, that it can actually make their lives easier.

Companies in high-technology industries like telecommunications have recently grasped the idea that they need to move from being technology-driven to being market-driven. AT&T's long-distance service, which attracted 31 million subscribers when it was launched in 1994, was closely based on the results of a customer survey which stressed the demand for something straightforward and intelligible. It was the most successful long-distance promotion in history.

At around the same time, Jack Welch declared that his company, General Electric, would concentrate on value-driven products because 'wherever you look, value is what people are buying'.

But how do your customers perceive value? What are their demands – voiced or unvoiced – that you will need to satisfy? As we have already noted, customers often don't know what they want until someone gives it to them. One of the best ways of finding out what they really want is to use the model I call the customer wheel (see diagram overleaf). At KPMG, we have applied this model for many of our leading clients.

We begin by assessing, or trying to imagine, customers' real needs and frustrations as they set about the routines or normal courses of action that bring them into contact with the company concerned. Let's look for a moment at the customer wheel as it applies to air travel, and we can observe the relevant stages in the cycle. These are:

- Reserve ticket
- Get to airport
- Check in
- Wait
- Board
- Fly
- Collect luggage
- Go to destination

We have seen earlier how British Airways and Virgin – with other airlines rapidly following suit – did much to ease the traveller's journey by reducing check-in queueing and providing comfortable lounges in which to wait. But business people don't like to wait. They want to be able to do business, or else relax completely. Sitting in a comfortable chair with a

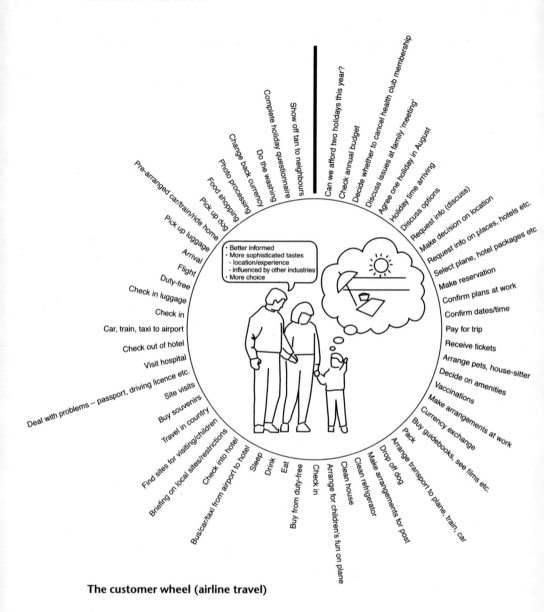

The customer wheel (airline travel)

newspaper may not be enough. Hence the recent proliferation of services available in the waiting lounges. Virgin's latest efforts are particularly impressive: elimination of check-in for business customers, direct delivery to departure gate, no charge for sending and receiving faxes, copying documents, even using PCs, sending e-mail messages and being able to surf the Internet. So comprehensive are the facilities at Virgin's executive lounge at Heathrow that people must be tempted to leave their own hectic offices early to get to the airport and do business – that is, if they don't want to unwind by practising their swing in the 'Golf Lounge'. Competition among airlines at the world's leading airports has intensified in this area, with an increasing number offering massage, manicures or other body treatments, or the use of well-equipped gyms.

The traditional airline view had always been that responsibility began with check-in and ended with luggage collection. Here again Richard Branson was the first to pursue the customer wheel all the way to the traveller's ultimate destination. Hence the motorcycle rides to central London – a bit of a gimmick, you might say, and certainly not a regular part of Virgin's service. But the free limousine from airport to destination is a gambit Branson has used round the world. When he introduced transatlantic flights to Florida, for instance, he chose to fly to Orlando – not least because it is the site of Disney World. At the same time, to cater for passengers who might want to go to Tampa on business, he provided a free limousine service all the way (about one and a half hours) from Orlando.

Applying the customer wheel to other business scenarios, you can identify points at which customers experience frustration. In some cases, it may be possible to develop an entirely new business in a previously unidentified area.

One of KPMG's clients, an energy company in a developing country, recently provided us with a challenge along rather different lines. The client wanted to build a gas factory, using leading-edge technology, but was not prepared to pay the going rate. The task seemed impossible. In the first place, the desired technology was available only in Europe or the US, and not within the client's budget. Secondly, we needed to send top-notch engineers and process specialists to the country in question; this would be costly, and some of the best people would not want to go. But we recognised the potential of a long-term relationship with this particular client in one of the world's growing markets, and set about trying to find a way round the problem.

Having employed the customer wheel to identify the true sources of frustration, we came to the following conclusions:

- 80 per cent of the functionality of a gas factory is standard, regardless of the client's specific requirements
- This functionality can be broken down into various component parts and dealt with in modules
- For each functional module we could easily identify ahead of time the suppliers and subcontractors who could provide the best quality at an acceptable price; then we could establish contracts that would guarantee the lowest possible purchasing cost
- We could apply the skills and knowledge of our brightest people to that 20 per cent of the project where they were most needed
- By more selective deployment of specialists, we could complete more projects with the same number of people, thereby reducing the cost of any single project.

Even if your company is not equipped to deal with a particular problem on the customer wheel, you may know of another organisation that could help. You don't have to do everything yourself. Why not call in outside help? If you've solved the customer's problem, you'll still get the credit, not to mention the commission. Your relationship with the customer will be stronger, and your future opportunities that much greater.

Eliminating customer frustrations brings us back to the bundling idea introduced in Chapter 2. Let's think about something from the custo-mer's point of view – house moving, for instance. Moving house can be hell, particularly when you have to go to different agents for the sale of your own house and the purchase of a new one, when you have to find a surveyor, a solicitor and finally a removals firm – not to mention amending your insurance arrangements, and possibly arranging a bridging loan with your bank. Many customers would happily pay a premium to kill all these birds with one stone – and, at last, there are a growing number of customer-conscious estate agents prepared to organise all of these aspects of moving house.

When it comes to buying cars, most customers are perfectly happy to pay a premium for one simple form of bundling – the hire-purchase agreement. Once you have identified the car you want to buy, but you don't have the cash to buy it immediately, you need to pay by instalments. In almost every case, you would be able to arrange a more advantageous loan direct from a bank or other financial-services provider. But the car salesman can arrange it all for you there and then – with the result that many of us sign straightaway, knowing that, even if it isn't the best interest rate available, it's not far out of line, we know we can make the payments, and that's one more thing we won't have to worry about. We willingly pay a premium for convenience.

Private banking contains an element of bundling, in that the banker takes responsibility for an entire portfolio, relieving the client of the need to monitor every single investment. Event-management companies are perhaps the most comprehensive current example of bundling. For instance, the list of items to consider when preparing for a ball following a wedding might include: the marquee, canapes, champagne, wine, dinner, breakfast, lavatories, band, disc jockey, valet parking, waiters, flowers, lighting, sound, insurance, balloons, wedding cake, photographers, tables, chairs, crockery, dance floor and where to put it. In an ideal world one phone call could take care of all of these things. And that ideal world is something that many party organisers are offering. Give us the job, they say, and we'll do all the phoning for you.

To be dealing with just one company is as convenient for the customer as it is profitable for the chosen company.

Bundling fails when the customer is no longer being put first, and when, like cross-selling, the bundling is done primarily for the convenience of the bundler. Airline travel can be a good example. Tour operators typically offer an organised sightseeing tour, with the airline ticket and accommodation included. Deals of this kind are popular because they are good value, and they relieve holidaymakers of the need to make decisions; the holidaymaker can simply relax and be entertained. But there are different kinds of travellers who like to make their own entertainment. They may use a tour operator to get an airline ticket at a good price, and they may like to arrange car hire at the same time. But it is most unlikely that customers of this kind will be interested in making hotel bookings for a number of days; instead, they will almost certainly arrange their own accommodation in several different places – that's why they hired the car! The holiday company that tries to sell as many of its products as it possibly can to all its customers regardless will soon come unstuck.

Few organisations have only one type of customer. So you need to think hard about the customers you have, and the customers you want. Then you can start to separate them into categories – but be careful: by categorising your customers, you must not dehumanise them in your own mind. People who talk habitually about customer bases and customer segments move all too easily into a world of abstractions where they have little or nothing to do with the living and breathing customers who are their lifeblood.

By using the customer wheel, we aim to find out what our customers really need. The next step is to find out what makes them loyal. If, by careful study, you can identify what makes your customers loyal, you can make real progress – because loyal customers buy more, take less corporate time, are less price-sensitive, bring in new customers, and have fewer acquisition costs. MBNA, the US credit-card provider, set out a simple credo in its 1993 annual report: 'We keep customers by exceeding their expectations every single time they come in contact with us.' Targets were set accordingly: the telephone to be answered within two rings, systems to be constantly available, and changes to customers' accounts to be made quickly and accurately. Results were posted daily, and employees rewarded when clients' expectations were exceeded. MBNA has calculated that a 5 per cent increase in customer retention increases company profits by 60 per cent five years later. In an article on 'loyalty-based management' published in the *Harvard Business Review* in 1993, F. F. Reichheld calculated that MBNA was losing customers at only half the industry rate.

If you develop a reliable value proposition for your customers, brand it if you can. A customer who acquires an initial fondness for, then loyalty to, a particular brand is a stakeholder par excellence – someone with an emotional commitment that makes them uniquely valuable.

The final step in meeting customer needs is to rework the customer relationship.

2 Shareholders

For many of our clients, shareholder pressure is one of the most constant, maddening and potentially destructive forces they have to cope with. If they ignore or disappoint the City, they can be destroyed overnight. Consequently, no sensible chief executive ignores the demands of shareholders. But capitulating to those demands can be every bit as destructive – even if death is slower.

To begin with, you must understand what shareholders are after. Put simply, they expect income from dividends and capital growth through increases in the share price. Some are prepared to take a risk in the hope of receiving higher growth; they are liable to sell quite quickly if their shares don't perform as they would like. Others want a secure return and may be content to receive lower than market rates if they are convinced of the value of their long-term investment. Companies cannot appeal to every kind of shareholder, and will usually need to decide at an early stage which kind they wish to attract.

Marks & Spencer, for instance, has no interest in short-term punters, and does not flinch from its long-term strategy when a spate of selling triggers a fall in the share price. The company's strategy is based on offering its shareholders consistent high growth and steady dividends over a number of years. It is confident of its value proposition for those long-term shareholders.

But identifying your preferred type of shareholder is the easy part. Now you need to create more value for your shareholders than the competition. AT&T decided that this was the key to its future success, and radically changed its priorities. As a functionally organised telephone company, it had previously regarded operating income as the main measure of performance. But from 1988 onwards the company began to concentrate more on markets, creating independent businesses with their own income statements and balance sheets. AT&T introduced the concept of 'value-based management' in 1992 and a year later linked its employees' pay to the creation of economic value for shareholders. This was done by using a measure of 'economic value' based on a combination of income after tax and the effect of exploiting assets. AT&T believes that market value is a truer reflection of the way a company performs than earnings per share, operating margins or return on equity. The company's managers also believe that this concentration on shareholder value fosters an entrepreneurial spirit by concentrating on returns over both short and long term.

The aim should be to co-evolve with your shareholders. This means good communication, openness and consistency. The common assumption that a shareholder's interest is purely financial is far too narrow. An increasing number of shareholders will no longer invest in businesses that they regard as unethical, or environmentally unsound. And many like to track their investment, experiencing the company's ups and downs in much the same way as sports fans follow the fortunes of their teams. The utterly dispassionate shareholder who buys or sells purely on a stockbroker's recommendation is becoming rarer.

Looking after today's discriminating shareholders is not easy. It means paying constant attention to their needs – which is just what one of the world's biggest hotel and catering groups failed to do when Forte succumbed to a £3.8 billion hostile takeover bid by Granada in January 1996.

The Italian Charles Forte had built up his empire with remarkable speed in the 1950s and 1960s; in addition to hotels and roadside cafés all over Britain, his company owned the George V in Paris and had narrowly failed on several occasions to buy control of London's Savoy Hotel, in which the company held a large stake. But by 1996 the Forte empire was in the hands of Sir Rocco Forte, son of the founder, and was seen to be suffering from a confusion of multiple brands, bloated headquarters and an irrational fixation with trophy hotels. Up popped Granada, with a 15 per cent share in Forte and a dynamic chief executive in Gerry Robinson, who claimed he could run the Forte empire much more efficiently.

The *Guardian* reported in December 1995:

At the heart of the argument is Granada's claim that Forte is an ill-managed chain of under-exploited assets. Sir Rocco has attempted to pre-empt these claims by showing that he had already sought to reduce debt by flogging off fringe assets. Progress is being made on moves to ginger up its management and make a clear demarcation of brands. That said, Sir Rocco has been outflanked by Granada's latest claims that it can squeeze another £100m per year out of the Forte business. Sir Rocco has yet to make any kind of meaningful response to the claims which must be making Granada's bid increasingly attractive to shareholders. An investment in Forte, after all, has underperformed the FTSE index by more than 20 per cent over the past five years.

Forte was forced into unveiling a demerger plan, a streamlining of brands, a change in management roles and a strategy to create profits of £100 million. It was too little too late. Granada came back with a further bid which included a special dividend for the benefit of tax-exempt institutions, with a cash alternative for those not exempt, and the shareholders voted in Granada's favour. So how had an institution like Forte allowed its recent shortcomings to negate so many decades of achievement in its shareholders' eyes?

In the first place, Forte had not been looking after its major share-holders. Mercury Asset Management, which had a 15 per cent stake, had been assiduously courted by Granada, and was clearly in the Robinson camp when the first takeover whispers began. The issues with which Granada confronted Forte in 1995 were not new ones, and, if Forte had listened to its shareholders five years earlier, it would have begun to revamp its management, streamline brands and make itself more profit-able. Confronted with the choice, shareholders were understandably far more impressed with the management credentials of Gerry Robinson than those of Sir Rocco Forte. Granada's offer, when it came, was just too good for shareholders to turn down.

3 Employees

In dealing with employees we are confronting both a stakeholder and a lever of change. In the last chapter we considered how to turn your people from being a barrier into becoming a lever of change. Now we need to set about shaping a value proposition for the employee-stakeholder.

Like shareholders, employees need a basic financial inducement to work for a company. But the financial package can often be a complicated one, and different employees will put a different emphasis on basic pay as against other rewards such as commission, share options, holiday entitlement and pension rights. There is a trend towards more flexible conditions. So what kind of employee do you want? At one extreme, there are finance houses that employ money-market traders for their energy and speed of thought, and pay them as lavishly as possible to pour all their energies into the fiercely competitive world of the trading floor. In the last chapter, we discussed why it is desirable to control these performers by taking account of risks taken as well as profits generated. Although money trading has become a more complicated business in the 1990s, with traders looking for more career structure, this is likely to remain essentially a young person's game. Like professional athletes, people in these jobs usually burn out after a few years. The trick for the employer is to bribe the fastest and brightest with whatever it takes so that they will make even more money for you. The motivation on both sides is overwhelmingly financial.

At the other extreme are the companies that seek to harness an employee's talents for as long as possible. Management consultancies, global corporations and government agencies are likely to come into this category. We rely on building up the knowledge capital of our organisation; that is why we recruit carefully, train extensively, and do our utmost to create a value proposition that will bind an employee to us. Every time a valued employee leaves, we lose a certain amount of knowledge.

Look at it from the stakeholder's point of view. Valued employers are those that add value to their employees by providing packages that combine pay, holidays, learning opportunities and job satisfaction. This kind of package enables an employee to lead the life he or she wants.

Trust is essential. The Eastman Chemical Company publicly declares its belief in honesty and integrity, fairness, trust, teamwork, diversity,

the wellbeing of employees, and citizenship. When the company embarked on a quality-improvement programme, it promised not to lay off
a single employee – even though everyone knew that the aim was to
enable fewer people to accomplish more. And it kept its promise. Ten
years after the programme started, Eastman's productivity had increased,
and its sales had risen by a similar amount. One of the main reasons that
those increased sales were achieved was that the company's employees
were able to identify completely with the company's commercial goals.
The interests of the two were indistinguishable.

This is a more or less revolutionary way of thinking. In most
organisations, employees are still essentially regarded as little more
than tools for the achievement of the company's aims. They should be
treated well, certainly, but not on a par. Perhaps natural human
competitiveness motivates most people to try to get to the top, then
stay there by keeping those below them in their places. It takes leaders of
vision to go against this prevailing flow, leaders like Jack Welch of GE,
who always wants to take his employees with him:

'Above all else good leaders are open,' says Welch. 'They go up, down
and around their organisation to reach people. It is all about human
beings coming to see things through a constant interactive process
aimed at consensus. My concept of loyalty is not "giving time", and in
turn, being shielded and protected from the outside world. Loyalty is an
affinity among people who want to grapple with the outside world and
win.'

If this is the kind of employee you want – one who will identify with
your company's aims and values – then your task is to shape a value
proposition that will promote affinity and encourage loyalty. Consultation and involvement are the keys.

GE, for instance, has developed a system of consultation known as
'Work Out'. Modelled on New England town meetings, Work Out invites
every employee in the company to come to meetings to discuss every

aspect of their work. The meetings are empowered to take decisions, to reform or abolish existing practices on the spot. Employees can see action matching rhetoric, and, perhaps even more important, they can see that it is the views of those most closely involved in the work that are likely to prevail. Seniority, by comparison, counts for little.

From the business's point of view, the most important thing is to build the loyalty of desired employees. As we have already discussed at the beginning of this chapter, there are positive and negative ways of building stakeholder loyalty. Let's just look, for a moment, at the dismal loyalty record of most investment bankers, traders, securities dealers and the like: the reason such people are easily poached by rival organisations is that this is an industry that manages its human resources in a one-sided manner, through benefits only, and usually in the form of performance-related bonuses. All a competitor has to do is to offer higher bonuses. Time-dependent benefits need to be added to the package. Stock options are one possibility, but for some reason most companies use this device almost exclusively for senior executives, leaving whole layers of rising stars exposed to temptations from outside.

When a company decides to go against the flow, it needs key personnel to stick around to implement the new strategy. We have already discussed the need to tackle switching costs as well as the basic value proposition, and in this case stock options or length-of-stay bonuses will increase switching costs and help to keep people longer, even if they go eventually. But there is one more subtle and more powerful loyalty card that a small number of enlightened organisations have learned to play: this is the Market Value Builder (MVB). The idea is to create an environment conducive to the maximum personal development – training courses, further education leading to MBAs or similar qualifications, rotation of roles, fast-track programmes for exceptionally talented performers, exciting postings abroad, and sabbaticals for the purpose of study, research or writing books. Such experiences help to build an employee's market value.

Why, you might ask, would anyone want to build an employee's market value and thereby make them more attractive to the competition? Why invest so much money in someone, only for another company to reap the rewards? Plausible questions, but short-sighted ones. Although the MVB method may result in occasional losses of highly rated personnel just as they were approaching their peak, most people will actually prefer to stay with an organisation that continues to boost their market value. Why would any sensible employee cast aside a job of this kind in favour of a less respected organisation where your market value might fall?

I don't know of any organisation that has consciously built a complete MVB programme as part of an employee-loyalty scheme. But there are many who have used MVB elements. The consultancy firm McKinsey encourages its brightest people to take sabbaticals so that they can research and write books and articles. In this way, they build the ideal career platform, both intellectual (their own publications) and practical (their work with McKinsey clients). McKinsey goes even further in its apparent philanthropy with an outplacement programme, helping those who wish to leave, by placing them in senior positions with clients or prospective clients. This has two interesting consequences: first, the firm now has many more powerful friends, who can bring in new business; secondly, the more successful placements it achieves, the more sought-after its employees become – and so more and more people want to work for McKinsey.

4 Suppliers

Truly enlightened organisations aim to achieve a similar affinity with suppliers, their fourth key stakeholder. And, sure enough, GE is increasingly including suppliers (and occasionally customers) in its Work Out meetings.

But why are suppliers so important? Because, if you can gain a measure of control over the quality, cost and reliability of your supplies, you will increase your control over the entire value chain, and thereby be able to offer better quality and value to your customers.

Suppliers have various requirements. They will always seek a measure of security, a guaranteed outlet for their goods or services – which you can probably provide if the relationship is strong enough. They may well have an interest in research and development that they could not afford to pursue on their own. And they need continuous guidance and encouragement if they are to play the fullest possible part in improving the efficacy of your value chain.

So don't just beat suppliers down to the lowest price they can bear and assume that because they need the business they will put up with your mean-mindedness. Why not ask them to come and have a look at your factory? They might be able to supply something you hadn't thought of. Your own product designers tend to overspecify in order to ensure the quality of the product. A chat with your suppliers might identify an alternative, perhaps cheaper or more readily available source of supply.

Avon Cosmetics, for instance, recognises the importance of good supplier relationships, and involves suppliers in regular discussions around its strategic plans and sales forecasts. Avon has developed the PAYU (Pay As You Use) system whereby the company holds stock on hand, but pays only as that stock is sold. The benefits to Avon are obvious: better cash flow, flexibility and lead times. But there are benefits to the suppliers too, as they can reduce their own stockholdings and delivery charges. The PAYU system is simply more efficient for everyone involved. Suppliers, although they don't get paid so quickly, are paid strictly on merit – so that they know instantly which products are selling and which are not, and can adjust production schedules accordingly. Above all, supplier and buyer communicate.

Companies are increasingly aware of the need to base such relationships on more than price alone. Quality is also discussed, but this remains an area where much more could be done by shared research and development. Nestlé is an example of a company that has involved its suppliers closely in its confectionery manufacture, and has made small but significant changes as a result. The construction industry, by contrast, remains to a great extent trapped in the traditional macho business culture that rewards managers and buyers who can screw their suppliers down to providing goods at the lowest possible price.

When the pressure is on, there will always be a temptation to 'get tough' with suppliers in the hope of improving profit margins. But such short-sighted tactics can easily backfire as disgruntled suppliers switch to more considerate business partners, or cut corners to compensate for their loss of revenue.

There is one further factor driving businesses into closer relationships with suppliers, and that is technology. When sophisticated systems have to be constantly updated with detailed information, there is an urgent need to communicate more closely with suppliers. And with communication the chances of mutually beneficial long-term relationships increase. We shall explore the development of those relationships in the next chapter.

5 Business managers

Business managers come into a different category from employees because of their specific responsibilities for the execution of strategy. We call them 'business managers' to distinguish them from middle managers, whose responsibilities are more limited; nonetheless, we want a category broader than chief executive, so that we can include leaders in various areas, operating at various levels – the heads of business units, for instance. As Bartlett and Ghoshal put it, 'In today's emerging information age, the critical scarce resource is no longer capital but knowledge, composed of information, intelligence and expertise. Knowledge becomes most valuable when controlled and used by those in the front lines of an organisation.' (*Changing the Role of Top Management*, Harvard Business Review, 1995). These are the people we are concerned with here.

Creating a value proposition for a business manager involves many of the same considerations as for an employee, but with a subtly different emphasis. To put it crudely, whereas the employee thinks in terms of work, the business manager thinks of a career. From the employer's point of view, pay and working conditions are the key issues for most staff. But for senior managers an issue of equal importance is career development. Value for such people, therefore, means prestige, recognition, fringe benefits and self-fulfilment, of which the last is probably the most important.

6 *Regulators*

Corporate behaviour is regulated by a variety of factors. There are official regulatory bodies, government departments, international trading agreements and lobby groups of all kinds. For our purposes, we are treating all these forces under this heading. Regulators, then, are those forces that work on businesses to make them conscious of the wider world beyond essential commercial transactions.

The Shell group of companies provides the perfect case study. 'Why is the world's most profitable company turning itself inside out?' asked *Fortune* magazine in August 1997. Shell had just led *Fortune*'s Global 500 in total profits for the third year in a row, earning no less than $8.9 billion in 1996. And yet Shell's chairman, Cornelius Herkstroter, had considered it necessary, as early as 1994, to embark on a corporate restructuring programme that shook this gigantic organisation to its core. Financial underperformance – low return on invested capital, to be precise – had convinced Herkstroter that all was not well. And, just as the restructuring began, the cracks started to show.

When Shell decided to sink Brent Spar, a derelict oil-storage platform, in the North Sea, the company had performed its usual checks for local reaction, and established that, as far as the oil industry in Scotland was concerned, there was no significant objection. It was in Germany, quite unexpectedly, that a campaign by militant environmentalists, brilliantly orchestrated by Greenpeace, suddenly gripped the public imagination. As Shell was reviled in print for its cavalier willingness to pollute the oceans, a few Shell petrol stations were firebombed, and forecourt sales in Germany slumped by 50 per cent.

As Robert Corzine noted in the *Financial Times*, the episode

> revealed the dangers of the old style of decentralisation; managers had never thought that a decision by a Shell operating company in one country could trigger violent attacks against a Shell company in another. It also caused widespread dismay among employees and high-lighted just how detached Shell management had become from the wider world.

Worse was to come. Within a few months, the military dictatorship in Nigeria, sustained by oil revenues managed on its behalf by Shell, executed the writer and activist Ken Saro-Wiwa, who had fought for the rights of the Ogoni people in his homeland against the depredations of the oilmen. Now Shell had blood on its hands as well as pollution. Public criticism was matched by intense self-criticism. In the words of Shell's former vice-chairman Sir John Jennings, 'We were bureaucratic, inward-looking, complacent, self-satisfied, arrogant . . . We were technocratic and insufficiently entrepreneurial.'

Within a few months, senior management had embarked on Myers-Briggs personality tests as well as a variety of team-building exercises, including climbing walls in the rain and digging earth at low-income housing projects. Word went out from the top that Shell people had to become aware not only of the concerns of customers, shareholders and the competition, but of how they were seen by the outside world. With a company with the global reach and wealth of Shell, almost any member of the public can plausibly claim to be a stakeholder, entitled in some measure to be able to regulate the company's behaviour. And that meant that it was incumbent upon every manager within Shell to communicate the company's concerns, priorities and policies to the wider world – and, where necessary, to justify its actions.

Shell's established staff were suddenly disestablished. In every department, people were required to reapply for their own jobs, which were advertised on the Shell-wide web. But the company's way of dealing with the outside world was changed even more dramatically. The old ways of making decisions were replaced by round tables, discussions with lobby groups, consultation, the sharing of dilemmas.

As if to confirm its radical change of heart, Shell withdrew in 1997 from the Global Climate Coalition, the oil-industry umbrella group that habitually lobbied for limits to environmental controls on its own activities. This was not pure altruism, but a realistic assessment of the need for different priorities in a changing world. As Henk Dijkgraaf, strategic development director for Shell International Exploration and Production, told a London conference on Oil and Money in November 1997: 'We live in a show-me world, where we have to earn our Licence to Operate day by day.' Perhaps there was a little of the old Shell immodesty in the title of Dijkgraaf's speech that day. He called it 'A Force for Good'. But he meant it.

I have treated environmental groups, local lobbyists and all the other organs of public opinion as 'regulator' stockholders. And the supremacy of such stakeholders even in such an overtly commercial industry as oil exploration is no illusion. On the contrary, it is the completion of a cycle. For the time has come when institutional investors ask the same questions about ethical corporate behaviour as lobby groups. Companies cannot afford to be blacklisted by Greenpeace, the Co-operative Bank, or any other organisation capable of influencing public opinion. Being environmentally aware and socially conscious is not just intrinsically desirable. It's an absolute requirement.

What Shell has been learning is that the way to provide value for regulators is to build compliance into your system – just as businesses learned to do with quality in the heyday of TQM. Britain's financial-services industry has learned a similar lesson even more belatedly, and at similar cost. The pensions-misselling scandal that disgraced many of the country's most prestigious insurance companies and financial institutions in the 1990s has cost those institutions at least £1 billion to put right. It would have cost a fraction of that if they had simply studied the 1986 Financial Services Act closely, talked to the IMRO regulator, and built in their own safeguards against overzealous salesmanship.

The trouble began in the summer of 1988, when personal pensions became available, encouraged by a government understandably worried about the strain of maintaining a state pension for a growing proportion of old people, funded by a declining number of working adults. Its extent was fully revealed six years later when the Securities and Investments Board published its report, entitled with apparent insouciance, *Pension Transfers and Opt-Outs – Review of past Business*.

In short, the scandal consisted of a clash between the greedy (commission-chasing salesmen) and the naïve (unsophisticated customers). First, people were told they would be better off with a personal pension than in their company scheme. After all, said the persuasive life-assurance salesman, company schemes are not that safe. 'You can retire earlier with a personal pension, perhaps with a larger pension, if the money is invested well.' Hundreds of thousands of people believed this and signed on the dotted line, while the salesman pocketed a fat commission.

Three or four years on, the customers found they had been misled. They had left a better pension scheme for a worse one. They and their families faced the loss of thousands of pounds of valuable benefits.

During this time, regulators made feeble attempts to restrain life companies by issuing 'guidance' that pension transfers were not always a good idea. Many life companies, not surprisingly, ignored the advice. 'Business was booming,' noted an editorial in *The Times*, 'and they weren't about to choke off the goose that laid the golden eggs.'

Eventually, regulators decided to act more decisively. The Securities and Investments Board's report was published showing that nine out of ten salesmen either had not bothered to get enough information to give sensible advice on transferring, or had given bad advice in the face of overwhelming evidence that someone should stay put.

'Poor advice has been given and that advice has to be paid for by the industry which gave the advice,' declared Andrew Large of the SIB. Pensions, said Large, had been sold 'improperly'. As John Monks, general secretary of the Trades Union Congress, commented, 'This whole sorry saga has soiled the reputation of companies that were once household names for probity.' Mick Newmarch, chief executive of the Prudential Corporation, was a case in point. What Newmarch did was not illegal, nor was he breaking Stock Exchange rules. But as the columnist Bernard Levin put it in *The Times*, 'Did he at any point stop to think what the public at large might think of him? And if he had done so, might he have thought again?'

In retrospect, it seems incredible that so many respected companies could simply turn a blind eye to salesmanship that went way beyond overzealousness into misrepresentation and outright fraud. Regardless of the presence of the regulator, couldn't the directors of these companies appreciate that what they were condoning was simply unethical? Or did the left hand simply not know what the right hand was doing? Either way, their behaviour was inexcusable. It was also typical. Typical of the laissez-faire attitude of directors whose companies were making profits, and who didn't really care why or how. 'If it ain't broke, don't fix it' would have been the attitude. This was the way the prevailing current was flowing in Britain's financial-services industry, and most people, even if they entertained the briefest doubts as to their employees' behaviour, just looked at their competitors and neighbours and said to themselves: 'Well, if he's doing it as well, I suppose it's all right.'

If any of them had had the courage and independence of mind to go against the flow, they would have thought not simply about the risks of unethical behaviour, but would have considered the regulator's remit, and asked themselves what they could do to provide a value proposition for that particular stakeholder. Thus apprised of the necessary steps, they would have taken the opportunity to turn compliance into codified best practice – and saved their reputations and a great deal of money besides.

As Chris Doyle pointed out in a 1996 article in *Business Strategy Review*, 'the regulation of competition is about promoting efficiency'. He makes the point that competing football teams need a referee, without whom they would not be able to trust one another not to play dirty. Without a referee, both teams would play as dirty as they could in order to win – but the cost in terms of injuries would rapidly become unacceptable. It is therefore in the interests of all the players that the game be played cleanly, in view of a referee who will punish dirty play. The regulator, like the referee, is actually acting in the best interests of businesses. And it is only the short-sighted businesses that fail to recognise this.

7 Strategic allies

Our final category of stakeholder echoes the title of this chapter, 'A new kind of competition'. As strategic alliances become more and more popular – the growth of electronic commerce makes them even more attractive – we find traditional notions of competition being turned upside down. For what do we see all over the world but competing companies, erstwhile deadly rivals, joining forces to enter new markets or improve their competitive position?

Thus BP and Mobil join forces in 1998 to grab a larger slice of Europe's

roadside petrol-station business. The deal makes sense for both operators, who were finding themselves stretched to cater for motorists with
comprehensive service stations. In this case, BP runs the petrol side,
while Mobil takes care of oil and other necessary accessories.

We find AT&T building a transatlantic undersea cable in collaboration
with three southern telecommunications companies in order to meet
demand that has almost exhausted the existing network. And most
recently we find the American company Carrier, the world's largest
maker of air conditioners, joining forces with the Japanese company
Toshiba to sell air conditioning in Europe and Asia. Toshiba Carrier, the
new $505 million company, to be launched in April 1999, provides a
further foothold for Carrier in an Asian market in which it already has
eight joint ventures. For Toshiba, whose air-conditioning business had
not made a profit for two years, the deal represented an opportunity, in
the words of Toshiba's president, Taizo Nishimuro, 'to achieve a
fundamental revision of our household electronics division and develop
our air-conditioning business globally'.

In a sense, this last example follows the long-standing practice of
businesses operating abroad, particularly in developing markets, where
the foreign company will often look for a joint venture with a local firm.
The local partner, maybe a state-controlled company, will probably have
the necessary connections, local knowledge and a willing workforce. A
joint venture carries far less risk. But Toshiba Carrier is about more than
that. Although the biggest prize from Carrier's point of view may be the
opportunity to penetrate the Asian market, Europe comes into the
equation too, and Carrier holds a majority stake in the marketing
operation in Britain, Thailand and Malaysia. In short, it is a global strategic
alliance of a kind that is being emulated all over the world every day.

Of course, strategic alliances are not a new idea. Just like companies
operating abroad, large companies operating within a single country will
often enlist the help of local partners – trusted suppliers, for instance, as

we saw earlier in this chapter. But the alliances being made every day in the new global marketplace are of a different order. Above all, the market now demands of businesses that they look at themselves and their competitors in a new light, and ask questions that may not have occurred to them a few years ago. Those questions may be along the following lines. Where is the next global market opportunity? Can our company meet this actual or prospective demand? Is there another company – or companies – that could help, regardless of whether they are competitors? What can each bring to the party? Is there a realistic prospect of mutual benefit?

Once the opportunity has been identified, your task, as with every other stakeholder, is to develop a value proposition. That means consulting your ally as soon as you have identified potential mutual benefit. Find out what they want, and if you can give it to them. If you don't, someone else may, and the opportunity will have gone.

Not that this is the easy part. Far from it. It is hard to develop a value proposition for someone who is, in all other respects, a competitor. How much can you tell them? How much will they be prepared to tell you? Can you trust them? Mightn't they take advantage? Any propensity to paranoia will be most unhelpful here. What is needed is a calm assessment of opportunities and interests.

Mutual gain is possible where

- the partners' strategic goals converge but there is no direct competition
- neither partner can make a sufficient impact by themselves
- each partner can learn from the other without sacrificing proprietary skills
- it is possible to develop a common culture

If mutual gain is the aim, it follows that only those areas that offer mutual gain should be included. Commercial confidentiality can be maintained over all matters outside the specific project. Now the challenge is to set up a project team with a common goal, and a shared respect for the other's interests.

To empathise with all these stakeholders, to appreciate their concerns, to think on their behalf, even to move your company alongside theirs for the maximum mutual benefit, requires an immense imaginative effort. It is all too easy to fall back into old habits, traditional demarcation lines between a company and its customers, shareholders, employees and suppliers. Nemesis will not be instant, but it will be sure. The fate of the unwary has been likened to that of the frog in boiling water – and it is an apt simile.

It has been observed that if a frog is placed in a saucepan of cold water, and that water is gradually heated to boiling point, the frog will not struggle, or try to escape from the pan. Instead, it finds the initial warmth comforting until its torpor is so complete that it surrenders blissfully to its fate. I believe the same process is useful for boiling crabs and lobsters – but I digress. The point is that, if you fail to cater for your stakeholders, you will suffer a similar fate. You may never be aware of having done anything wrong. Your product may seem to be as good as ever, your internal processes efficient. As your staff strive to protect and reassure you, you may not even hear any complaints. While you remain content, like the frog in the warming water, your unseen competitors will quietly turn up the gas.

Awareness is the first essential. But then comes the tricky task of prioritising your stakeholders. For one thing is certain: you will never be able to please all of them at once.

Your priorities depend on the maturity of your business. A young business is concerned primarily with customers. Mature businesses depend just as much on the quality of their management and employees.

Your priorities also depend on the industry you are in. Manufacturers of cigarettes or nuclear-power plants may live or die by order of various regulators. In other industries, regulation is minimal.

Look at where you are and where your industry is, and you will usually be able to decide which stakeholders are the most important. Having decided where your priorities lie, you must then explain your decisions to every affected stakeholder. If you explain fully, you may be able to satisfy your stakeholders even though you can offer them nothing. Every stakeholder will understand that you can't afford to lose customers – or staff, or suppliers. And few stakeholders will hold it against you if you comply with a regulator when the alternative is to have your business closed down. But, when stakeholders are deceived, they may never forgive.

In the business mainstream, where the traditionalists talk openly about management's right to manage, and privately about screwing down suppliers or pulling the wool over the regulator's eyes, they think openness in corporate governance is just PR. It isn't, as I hope I have shown.

CHAPTER 5 – DIGEST

Reworking relationships

Key message:

Every business depends on the relationships it develops with its various stakeholders. In an age of discontinuous change, you have to be outgoing, responsive and aware, prepared to rework your external relationships.

Why?

Because in the information society, traditional relationships give too narrow a perspective. Stay where you are and you will miss opportunities.

What?
- How not to do it: banks
- How to do it: involve the customer
- Different routes to the customer
- Managing networks
- New roles for employees
- Active shareholders
- Suppliers as partners
- When competitors become allies

So what?

So look at your business relationships, as the means of forging new futures.

CHAPTER 5

Reworking relationships

In the last chapter we considered the parable of the boiling frog and the need to adjust to a new kind of competition. As mature businesses make these adjustments, they find that many old assumptions no longer apply. In particular, relationships with stakeholders are changing utterly. When it was assumed that the competition was the enemy, commercial confidentiality was vital, and secrets were kept within a small executive group. Customers were treated like theatregoers, and never allowed to see behind the scenes; shareholders were given only carefully approved information; employees and suppliers were treated with similar suspicion, as security risks.

But today, when so many old hierarchies have been demolished, and knowledge is communicated instantly from corner to corner of the globe, secrets are harder to keep – and so are the old certainties and distinctions. Customers become partners, employees become shareholders, and competitors become allies. If you are content to drift in the mainstream, your business relationships may change, but others will be changing them for you, and you will have no control over your destiny. If, and only if, you go against the flow, confident in your business vision and open-minded about the relationships you may develop along the way, will you be able to choose the relationships you want.

Our task in this chapter is to take a closer look at our relationship with each stakeholder, to define, capture and shape that relationship. The ability to do this is one of the key factors that differentiate winners from losers. We must begin by separating ourselves from mainstream thinking. The traditional approach assumes that, for almost every kind of business, the key relationship is with the person who pays you. If you sell your goods wholesale, your key relationship is with the retailer. If you sell your services, your key relationship is with the buyer. This view is hopelessly narrow. Worst of all, it makes you utterly dependent on this primary relationship. If you sell to retailers or buyers who are hit by a slump in demand, that slump will hit you just as hard.

There is a lot more to business today than buying and selling. Imaginative or unusually powerful companies can often exploit two relationships at once, selling their goods to retailers, while simultaneously mounting a massive advertising and marketing campaign to capture the allegiance of the end-consumer – thus enlisting the consumer's help in putting pressure on the retailers to buy their products. Over the ensuing pages, we shall examine a number of different companies and businesses, and learn how to define, capture and shape each stakeholder relationship in turn, so that we acquire sufficient control to be able to make things happen the way we want. The consumer relationship is without question the most important, so that is where we begin.

Defining the customer relationship

At the most basic level, a supplier of goods or services decides what to purvey, then depends on finding a sufficient number of customers in order to become a viable business. By improving the product or service in some way, the business can then aim either to charge more, or find more customers. This simplistic approach is no longer adequate for the challenges of today's global markets. And yet there are mature businesses, even industries, that seem not to have progressed beyond this kind of narrow definition.

In Chapter 1, we discussed the problems of banks. Banks, like all too many corporate institutions, have found it almost impossible to rid themselves of the notion that there are immutable divisions in the world of business, like laws of nature. There are banks, insurance companies, department stores, supermarkets and so on – and these are distinct types of organisation performing quite different functions within the retail sector. Banks, according to the traditional definition, provide financial products and services. Their job, therefore, is to make those products and services as good as they can, while containing their costs and making their processes as efficient as possible in order to achieve maximum profitability. Nonsense. They are retailers, and in the twenty-first century they will survive or perish depending on their ability to exploit business relationships, above all with customers. It was this failure of definition that led to so many banks concentrating on their products and internal processes when they should have been asking themselves what their customers really wanted. We remember Dick Kovacevich of Wells Fargo, mentioned in Chapter 2, as an honourable exception.

Now let's consider a different way of looking at the customer relationship. Disney, one of the outstanding business success stories of the twentieth century, was founded on the belief that a business relationship with a customer was not one-dimensional. Disney does not simply peddle cartoons, or amusement parks. Disney has always offered a fantasy – an alternative world in which the customer may choose to escape. But that fantasy can come alive only when the customer makes an imaginative effort.

Dumbo and Bambi captivated millions round the world because, wherever the films were shown, moviegoers got their handkerchiefs out. Without the participation of viewers, without their emotional reaction, Disney's creations would have been worthless. Similarly, the rides at Disney World work only because the customers shriek and squeal with terror, excitement and delight. This has been described as 'the Experience Economy' – the formula whereby the supplier provides only half the product, and the customer provides the other half. The idea is capable of many different applications.

By bringing in half the product and relying on the customer for the other half, a business can create a new relationship. The Swedish company IKEA, for instance, does not believe primarily in making something of value for its customers, but in mobilising those customers to create value for themselves. By producing simple items of furniture, which can be painted, decorated or combined with other parts and made into more complicated pieces, IKEA aims to give its customers a buzz – a desire to go on making home improvements. IKEA's own products have less value-added content than those of many of their competitors. This makes them cheaper, and when customers can save money, discover new ways of doing things, customise their homes and feel better about themselves in the process, they have discovered a different kind of value altogether. IKEA becomes less a shop than a facilitator, while customers take on roles traditionally filled by tradesmen – fitters, joiners, carpenters and the like. The provider/customer relationship has been redefined, and the two are bound together in ways that promise new kinds of mutual benefit.

The French holiday company Club Med is an example of a company that went in the opposite direction. Discovering that a large number of holidaymakers did not want freedom, excitement and adventure so much as safety, order and routine, Club Med designed holiday packages that were rigorously standardised. Club Med resorts are usually sited so far away from towns or other holiday centres that there are no rival attractions within reach. The daily entertainment is carefully choreographed and administered by representatives known as *Gentils Organisa-teurs*. Money is converted into counters. Mealtimes and seating plans are decided by the GOs. Club Med holidaymakers relax and enjoy them-selves, secure in the knowledge that, for the duration of their holiday, they have no decisions to make, no doubts, no dilemmas, and no choice. This is the customer – supplier relationship turned on its head, with the supplier largely in control – albeit with the customer's explicit acquies-cence.

Other businesses find their customers determined to exercise their right to choose. As a result, they change their emphasis from product to service. When the American company Xerox decided to move away from being a supplier of office equipment, and reposition itself as 'The Document Company' – a company that provides a comprehensive document-handling service – its customers were the first people it called upon for help. Joint ventures were set up with Toshiba and Jetform to develop appropriate software. A colour-printing venture was undertaken with Fuji. And, in partnership with IBM, Xerox set about developing new uses of digital technology. Similar projects were undertaken with fifty of Xerox's leading clients, including AT&T, Hewlett-Packard, Compaq, Andersen Consulting, Ernst & Young, Microsoft and Oracle.

In such different ways, these very different companies have arrived at entirely new definitions of the customer relationship and it has been their willingness to defy convention, to go against the flow, that has enabled them to rethink the nature of their business. In most cases, a new lease of life has been the result.

Capturing the customer relationship

The next step is to capture the customer relationship, and there are many different ways of doing this. A moment ago, we looked at Xerox as an example of redefining the customer relationship. Now let's look at Canon, one of Xerox's most successful competitors, in the different context of actually capturing customers. Canon went against the flow by taking a different route. Distributing through dealers rather than through its own sales force, outsourcing maintenance, and selling rather than leasing its machines, the new arrival managed to avoid head-on conflict with the market leader, Xerox. But Canon's most crucial decision was not to target conventional corporate buyers but to go direct for the end-user, aiming its entire marketing campaign at secretaries, department heads and private individuals. Canon rapidly acquired a substantial market share while expanding the total market.

In the hunt for customers, you might think that banks have a head start, having a huge number of customers already virtually captive. They know their names, addresses, ages and financial circumstances. They even have a list of their daily transactions. But instead of using this information to anticipate their customers' needs, to make their lives easier – and thus capture them for the long term – all too many banks allowed themselves to be perceived more and more as organisations that existed to exploit their customers, with unjustifiable charges and apparently inflexible systems and procedures. As they moved their staff around with increasing frequency, closing branches all the while, the friendly bank manager became a mythical figure of the distant past.

The biggest indictment of the banks' complacency was that in the last decade of the twentieth century it was the supermarkets that showed them how it should be done, getting to know their customers in such a way that they could anticipate their needs. Their chosen instrument was the loyalty card, issued free to any customer prepared to sign up. Nothing could have been simpler. Existing customers signed up almost immediately when they realised that using the card would enable them to enjoy discounts on all sorts of goods. But the real value of the loyalty card was to the retailer. By monitoring the use of loyalty cards, supermarkets began to track their customers' behaviour, finding out when they shopped, what they bought and what they didn't buy, and how they wished to use their time. Standard procedure for professional kidnappers, of course. And let's not be precious about this: if you want new business, you should use every stratagem you can (within the law, of course) to acquire the information that will enable you to capture it.

Armed with this vital information, supermarkets offered new products, changed their opening hours, redeployed their staff, changed their displays and redesigned their stores. And, of course, they started to dabble in financial services, aware that they were acquiring a relationship of trust with their customers that many banks, which had always had this kind of information but hadn't known how to use it, could only envy. Loyalty cards had one other benefit: they fostered loyalty – in precisely the manner we discussed in the last chapter, by increasing switching costs. Why would any customer want the hassle of switching from a retailer offering more and more of what they really wanted, losing all their loyalty bonuses and having to start from scratch?

It wasn't only supermarkets that used these techniques. Other new entrants to the financial-services market were just as inventive. GE Capital is an outstanding example, with Virgin, almost inevitably, sticking its oar in. In Britain, the insurance company Direct Line put its established rivals to shame by offering comprehensive insurance policies over the phone, at lower cost. And there were banks that sharpened up their act – not least because they suddenly realised that they were no longer indispensable. Decades, even centuries, of being big fish in the financial mainstream were no guarantee of survival beyond the end of the twentieth century.

From the supplier's point of view, there are two main routes to the customer – business-to-business and direct-to-consumer. These form the various sides of the retail triangle. The left- and right-hand sides of the triangle represent the business-to-consumer relationship, while along the bottom we see the business-to-business route. Your key relationships will depend on which route you take – although you may well choose to explore both simultaneously.

The retail triangle

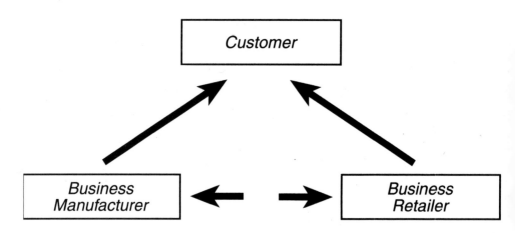

It is by no means essential that a business's main relationship should be with the people who pay it. Coca-Cola, for instance, secures its revenue entirely from wholesalers and retailers, who pay a certain amount for the concentrate, which they then convert into the drink the public buys in traditional glass bottles, cans or large plastic. But Coca-Cola scarcely has to cultivate that business-to-business relationship. Such is the drink's popularity that the public demand a certain amount, and retailers simply can't afford not to stock it.

Intel, the computer-chip company, is an even more interesting case study here. No question about Intel having a relationship with the consumer, who has been the object of one of the most phenomenally successful advertising and marketing campaigns in the history of computer technology. During the 1990s, the words 'Intel inside' and 'Intel pentium processor', associated with those few catchy notes of electronic music, became imprinted on the brains of consumers everywhere. I write as one of the brainwashed: so convinced was I by the marketing that I doubt if I would have taken seriously any PC that did not display the 'Intel Inside' logo in the corner of its screen.

But this extraordinary marketing campaign, which effectively hijacked the customer relationship from the PC makers, was part of a two-pronged strategy. The other prong consisted of convincing the makers of PCs that the Intel chip was the best, and persuading them not to sell their PCs with any other chip (despite there being powerful rival chip makers out there, led by IBM). Intel's task in this respect was made a great deal easier by the fact that the marketing campaign had persuaded consumers to put their own pressure on the PC makers. If we look again at the diagram we can see how Intel pushes its product out towards the consumer via the PC manufacturers, while simultaneously pulling the consumer in via its own marketing.

Others had done it before Intel, of course. Ask people for a name to associate with stereophonic sound, and the answer will usually be Dolby. Ask them about quartz watches, and most will say Seiko. These are words that go together, as with Wrigley's chewing gum or Gillette razors. The marketing has been so successful that the retailer is under pressure to stock these products from both the supplier and the customer.

Dell Computer, by contrast, opted for a single-pronged strategy, selling direct to the consumer – also with considerable success. Dell was one of the first PC makers to opt for the Intel chip, and, having done so, was able to turn Intel's marketing to its own advantage by trading on the reputation of the new wonder-chip. By cutting out dealers, Dell has been able to keep its prices down, while nurturing a relationship with customers that has produced a remarkable degree of customer loyalty. Despite its direct relationship with its customers, Dell does not actually man its own switchboards or deliver its own products. Those tasks are outsourced to other specialist service providers. Dell's is a delicate balancing act, because if the company makes a mistake the customer may look elsewhere for advice – and, having obtained good advice from another quarter, will be understandably reluctant to return to a company like Dell that operates in such exclusive fashion.

It may be partly because of this inherent precariousness of the direct-to-consumer relationship that most large businesses opt for the business-to-business, professional-to-professional route. But there may be a more fundamental reason: it is easier dealing with fellow professionals, particularly if that is the way you have always done business in the past. The received wisdom is that we should concentrate on our business customers first and foremost; they are the specialists in dealing with the end-consumer – and so they should be, considering how long they've been doing it. We shouldn't get involved – it's not our forte. We're a business-to-business company, and we should stick to that.

Apart from being that familiar seductive pull of the mainstream, this reasoning is quite simply fallacious. The maker of a product is often far better qualified to sell it than the retailer. Direct-to-consumer relationships may not be easy, but business-to-business relationships can be every bit as tricky. Just ask the strategists at Pepsi-Cola, which tried to launch its product in South Africa, only to find that shops and stores, although nominally independent, were actually bound to Coca-Cola by virtue of having installed Coca-Cola refrigerators. Ice-cream manufacturers the world over have been quick to grasp this essential tool in controlling the business-to-business relationship, offering to install refrigerators in shops in return for a commitment not to sell their rivals' products. Castrol, which makes oil, maintains a similar stranglehold on its retailers. This is a classic example of first-mover advantage, which springs from a willingness to lead, not follow. If you allow yourself to be sucked into the mainstream, you cannot lead, only follow.

Shaping the customer relationship

Having captured your customers, what do you do next? The next stage, shaping the customer relationship, is perhaps the most vital of all. Sales techniques may have evolved in a myriad different ways over the centuries, but it is only relatively recently that organisations have learned about the importance of turning new customers into loyal customers. There are still businesses that allow high-pressure salesman-ship to dominate, with the result that disillusionment often sets in soon after the sale, and repeat business is reduced to a minimum. The double-glazing industry is a prime example – an industry that offered an instant solution to the perennial domestic problem in cold or damp climates of rotting wooden window frames and draughts. Throughout the 1960s and 1970s, double-glazing salesmen were allowed to run amok in the suburbs of northern Europe and the US. Disillusionment set in as people gradually realised that double glazing not only destroyed the look of most houses, but had the effect of drawing attention to other defects in any house of a certain age. It was, as any biblical scholar would know, like pouring new wine into old bottles ('bottles' in biblical times were actually skins, which deteriorated with age). The double-glazing sales-man has become an international figure of ridicule – and deservedly so.

As we discussed in the last chapter, enlightened business leaders have learned to concentrate not so much on the quick sale as playing the loyalty card – loyal custom being so much more profitable than one-off business. But how? Customisation is one method.

Even fixed products and services, which sell at a certain price depending on their size, capacity, degree of craftsmanship and aesthetic quality, can be customised. With luxury cars, for instance, it is becoming common for customers to be given the basic shell of a car, then invited to choose the upholstery, dashboard, steering wheel, sound system and all sorts of other enhancements from a variety of options. By the time the customer has finished, the car is almost as individually furnished as a studio flat. As customisation becomes increasingly significant, the product itself has limited intrinsic value; a substantial portion of its value depends on what it can do for a particular customer. IKEA's products belong a little further along the product/service spectrum, while Disney's fantasy world belongs still further along. There is nothing intrinsically desirable about being at Disney's end of the spectrum, or at the other end. The point is to be aware of the possibilities, and be prepared to rework your relationships.

Shaping the customer relationship usually involves others apart from you and your customer. Business-to-business relationships usually depend on networks. If you can create your own network, so much the

Customisation: climbing closer to the customer

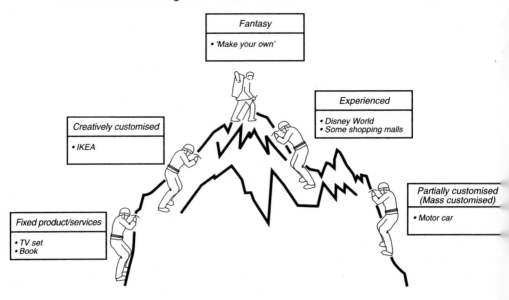

better, but this is not an opportunity available to most businesses. More to the point, you should aim to be critical to the functioning of a network – the essence of the theories of 'network centrality' and 'nodal organisation'.

Let's return to Intel for a moment. Having captured a virtual monopoly in its field within a year or two of combining its direct marketing campaign with its traditional relationship with manufacturers, Intel was faced with the opportunity to shape its relationship with end-consumers. The obvious method would have been simply to go on proving that Intel chips were the best, relying on word of mouth and the evidence of millions of satisfied customers to spread the word round the globe. But Intel gambled for higher stakes and continued to develop its chips, creating a new-generation model every year or so, capable of fulfilling an ever-greater range of tasks. As soon as the premium profits had been harvested from customers demanding the latest technology, Intel licensed mass chip reproduction and launched its next generation – a strategy of built-in obsolescence. And, just in case a rival enters the market with a superior product, Intel ensures that it has at least two generations of chip 'ready to market' (Source: *Fortune*, 23 June 1997).

Like most effective monopolies, Intel's market position has ended up by restricting consumer choice. An area for the US's antitrust legislators to think about, perhaps, but also an outstanding example of a company leveraging a customer relationship to the point where it was no longer obliged to follow the mainstream, but had obliged others to follow its own flow.

At around the same time, Compaq took a rather different approach. Aware that the computer industry was entering a deflationary phase, Compaq decided it had to provide a lower-priced product to sell at a discount compared with its main offering. 'If all goes well,' explained Peter Martin in the *Financial Times*, 'high-end customers keep buying the main product. Those motivated by price trade down, of course, but that is better than losing them to the competition. Volumes stay up and – if the low-end product is designed properly – margin is undamaged.' Martin particularly admires those companies in the electronics-based industries that manage to keep innovating with new high-end products, while keeping old lines going in tandem. 'This broadens a brand's shelf presence, retains loyal customers not ready to move, and provides an instant lower-price spoiler line, to fend off cut-price competitors.' Versatility of this kind is essential if we are to shape the customer relationship through good times and bad.

Reworking supplier relationships

If you can rework your relationships with customers in this way, why not with other stakeholders? In the automotive industry, for instance, large manufacturers have sought for some time to tie their component suppliers to them by a series of arrangements for mutual advantage. They buy components exclusively from a certain supplier, whom they also help with research and development. In return, the supplier is likely to opt for a longer-term contract at an agreed price that makes it very much easier for the manufacturer to control costs. With the kind of factory visits and exchanges of information that we encountered in the last chapter, manufacturer and supplier effectively pool their assets and liabilities until they become mutually dependent.

But this has to be a genuine meeting of minds. If you want maximum benefit from the relationship, you have to be as open with your suppliers as you want them to be with you. You know that, to provide the best possible products and services, it is not enough merely to deal with the retailer who buys from you: you have to know something about the end-consumer. So why would you restrict yourself to knowing your supplier, while remaining ignorant about your supplier's supplier? These individual relationships do not exist in isolation. Where does your supplier get his goods or materials from? The more you know about such things, the better. If you are to exploit your business opportunities to the full, you must know as much as possible about the entire chain from source supplier to end-customer. In the same way, if you want maximum value from your suppliers, you should be prepared to share with them your entire value chain. The more they know about your customers' requirements, the better.

All of this is easier said than done. In practice, conflicts are bound to arise. Say, for instance, your supplier takes pride in a particular product, but your customers tell you that they prefer something else. Human nature is such that many of us will try to avoid conflict, and choose not to mention such tricky matters. We will simply look for another supplier. Understandable, but time-consuming and counterproductive. Protecting any of your stakeholders from unpalatable truths only encourages them in misguided activities, and makes their long-term viability less likely. You may not always achieve an identity of interest, but you should certainly try.

Relationships between manufacturers and dealers have tended to follow a similar pattern, with service arrangements bringing both parties to an identity of interest that makes it difficult for others to intervene. Increasingly, however, the much greater financial clout of the manufacturer has made independent dealers an exception to the rule. Most of the major manufacturers also own dealerships, which ensure that their products find their way to the consumer. One way and another, the link from basic component and bodywork supplies to retail sales to motorists has become almost unbreakable in many cases.

A few years ago, an airbag manufacturer came to our business-transformation unit and asked for help to penetrate this increasingly impenetrable market. We undertook a thorough feasibility study, and reported back. Our advice was not to proceed. Unhappily, the client spurned this advice, and was obliged to abandon the project five years later. I mention this not for trumpet-blowing purposes, but to highlight the effectiveness of this kind of networking. By redefining relationships within their industry, motor manufacturers have substantially raised the barriers to imitation – one of the key goals of any business.

On a smaller scale, countless businesses have established partnerships with their suppliers that offer increasing opportunities for mutual benefit. Marks & Spencer, which has always set great store by the quality and reliability of its suppliers, has gradually refined its relationships so that it uses fewer individual suppliers, but relies more and more on those it really trusts. Northern Foods is an excellent example, a food producer that has gradually concentrated more and more of its business with Marks & Spencer to the exclusion of several other retailers. The advantage for Northern Foods is that it supplies an outstanding retailer able to charge higher prices than many of its rivals; furthermore, Marks & Spencer is such a respected brand with so many outlets – not to mention being an outstandingly well-run company – that there is minimal risk attached to supplying such a company almost exclusively. From Marks & Spencer's point of view, doing a substantial part of its business with one reliable supplier cuts down on administration and shortens the supply chain. The network is completed by a third partner, Christian Salvesen, which supplies the logistics services.

By contrast, the construction industry in Europe and the US is one where hardly any such effective networks exist. Such is the macho, hard-hat culture that few building firms look beyond the price issue to take a broader view, to consult and involve all the others who provide value to the end-customer. As a result, the industry is in a sad state. It is a different story in Japan, where civil-engineering firms have created a new model for project management.

Traditionally, major civil-engineering projects are won by large companies which then delegate various parts of the project to specialist subcontractors. When building a bridge, for instance, they will engage a firm that specialises in underwater construction. That firm may have its own geologists, divers and engineers; but it will probably subcontract other services such as transport, labouring and catering. Meanwhile, in another part of the project, the specialist road-building firm is deploying its own engineers, tarmac makers and road layers, while subcontracting many of the same ancillary services such as transport, labouring and catering. In many instances, the same labourers or caterers are employed and re-employed several times over by different subcontractors – each of which, naturally, adds a percentage to its charge to the main contractor. There is duplication, inefficiency, and extra cost to the main contractor.

Under the Japanese model, the main contractor may do less of the pure civil-engineering work, but will retain control of every part of the project. Project management becomes the name of the game rather than civil engineering, as the main contractor directly hires single firms of caterers, labourers and hauliers, and uses perhaps only four or five subcontractors in all. Cost control is hugely improved, and the entire project is far more likely to be completed on time, and within budget.

Reworking relationships with employers and managers

The involvement of employees and management is another area in which macho attitudes continue to hold businesses back. This is a classic problem of definition. Take the old-fashioned notion of 'management's right to manage'. In many cases, this is simply an excuse for keeping the workforce in the dark while those at the top try to stitch together deals of dubious value or effectiveness. It is a failure of trust that springs from insecurity, and the fear that, if you tell your staff what is really going on, they won't respect you any more. The truth, of course, is that if you are that insecure you don't deserve to be running a company. Redefine your relationship with your employees in terms of partnership, and make a genuine attempt to create value propositions for those employees. Having captured them, you must then shape the relationship in a way that ensures that everyone is committed to fulfilment of the same vision.

A common problem arises from the division of labour that is inevitable in any large organisation. Buyers, for instance, only rarely have much contact with their colleagues in marketing. And yet such contact can be enormously instructive. If buyers don't know what the company's customers really want, how can they communicate that to the suppliers? Just as we identified the need to understand the entire value chain from supplier to end-customer, so we need to ensure that everyone within our organisation has the same understanding.

This kind of openness, both within and outside your organisation, is a risk. There is always the possibility that one of your employees will be poached by a rival, and will reveal all the working methods that have helped you sustain your competitive edge. But it is a risk worth taking, because the alternative – misunderstandings and blockages in the system that will in time cause your organisation to atrophy – is so much worse. Besides, if you set your standards high enough, and reach them most of the time, why would anyone want to leave?

It is significant that News Corporation, Rupert Murdoch's global media business, uses its top management with rare imagination. Instead of keeping people in traditional management silos, News Corporation uses troubleshooting management teams whenever it embarks on a major new venture, whether it be with Star TV in China, or with the marketing of *The Times* in London. The best people are used where they are most needed, not where their seniority has placed them, and they often have a galvanising effect on the local people they work with.

Getting the best out of people is a preoccupation at my firm, as in most management consultancies. To this end, KPMG has adopted a ten-point 'Values Charter', which stresses the importance of sublimating personal ambition to corporate goals, sharing knowledge, respecting others, listening and learning. All very worthy, you might say, and, of themselves, these 'values' could be no more than window dressing. Nonetheless, the fact that at the very least we pay lip service to them makes it easier for everyone to feel part of the same project. At best, they redefine our relationships with each other, and make us better able to develop new relationships with our stakeholders.

Reworking alliances

We discussed strategic allies in the last chapter, as one of our stakeholders, and the basic concept is pure common sense. No single business can do everything, and, if there is an opportunity to penetrate new markets by allying ourselves with another company, we are foolish to ignore it. But in recent years the willingness of former competitors to join forces, and the readiness with which industry boundaries are crossed, have created an entirely new business atmosphere. It is as if several rival gangs had been shipwrecked, their weapons and colours washed away by the sea. In their new circumstances, struggling to survive as they make their way to shore, then learning a new way of life on a desert island, such people would abandon many of their former loyalties. They would redefine their relationships, and a new hierarchy would emerge based on strength, skill, intelligence and resourcefulness. Many of the old skills would be irrelevant, and new skills would come to the fore.

In the new business world, which may well resemble a shipwreck for those tied to the old ways, it is up to every business to consider its own strengths and weaknesses in certain markets, then look at rival outfits and see if some skills might be complementary. We have already seen how banks have been outmanoeuvred by supermarkets in exploiting customer relationships. In these circumstances, what could be more sensible than for a bank to seek a supermarket's help? It made sense for the Royal Bank of Scotland, which joined forces in 1997 with the supermarket chain Tesco to set up Tesco Personal Finance, just as the Bank of Scotland (not Royal) teamed up with J. Sainsbury. In the Tesco–RBS deal, Tesco benefited from RBS's expertise in areas like risk pricing for loans and credit cards; the bank also provides call centres and back-office support. At the same time, RBS was able to benefit from Tesco's ceaseless inventiveness in merchandising, product design and winning new customers.

Not all such alliances work. A previous link between Tesco and National Westminster bank foundered, according to Christopher Brown-Humes in the *Financial Times*, because of NatWest's concern about Tesco's banking ambitions. Brown-Humes is sceptical about the long-term prospects of the Tesco–RBS link. But this does not mean it is not a good idea. These are, after all, not love matches but marriages of convenience.

There are multiple marriages, too – like Iridium, a company formed by an international consortium of the world's leading telecommunications and industrial companies. Indeed, the very words 'world' and 'global' seem patently inadequate when discussing a business based, more or less literally, in outer space. For Iridium is providing wireless services via satellite, so that its customers can use a single phone number to communicate on existing cellular networks.

Not only was Iridium set up as a result of unprecedented co-operation between a host of different telecommunications and systems-management companies normally more used to treating each other as competitors: having appeared as the biggest conceivable threat to terrestrial mobile-phone operators, it has now emerged as a partner.

'I changed the strategy a month after taking over,' its chief executive, Ed Staiano, told the *Financial Times* in June 1998. 'I knew straight away that it did not make economic sense to compete with cellular, which would be able to beat us on capacity, as well as pressure us on price.'

Within eighteen months, Iridium had signed agreements with more than two hundred mobile operators in eighty countries. Many of those signatories acquired shares in Iridium, and several of the larger investors took seats on the board.

But we do not have to venture into outer space to find examples of relationships being redefined. When the game itself can change, we see more and more alliances between traditional competitors. Oil companies are a good example. Whereas the traditional game involved companies competing with each other all the way from exploration and production rights to big industrial contracts and petrol-pump sales, in recent years relationships have been transformed. BP and Mobil have formed an alliance to run service stations throughout Europe in tandem. Shell and Exxon have engaged in asset swaps in South America. Everywhere, companies have been looking to balance their exposure. Alliances such as these are turning what used to be perceived as competitive games with winners and losers into games where there need be no losers – the 'win-win situations' so beloved by management consultants.

As we have seen in previous chapters, an increasing number of companies, particularly in retail, are moving away from the idea of simply providing a product or service in take-it-or-leave-it fashion. Instead, they often invite the customer to have a say in the detailed form of the product. On the business-to-business front, we are moving away from the kind of products and services that can easily be imitated, and hence commoditised, to bundled solutions that address the customer's real concerns. From there, we are learning to move towards the idea of full partnership with the customer – sharing risks and rewards and each bringing a part of the answer. As customers become more sophisticated and more demanding, this trend will accelerate, as will the competition.

Back to the customer

However your relationships develop, controlling the customer relationship always remains the key. Ideally, we should try to go further, until we effectively own the customer. This does not mean that your business needs to be vertically integrated, merely that you should control the channels of communication and business, so that you become indispensable to the customer.

Just because you have to use someone else's network does not mean you have to lose that control. The Internet is rapidly becoming the network through which countless thousands of businesses are contriving new opportunities every day. At the time of writing, Internet traffic is doubling every hundred days. In the next chapter, we shall consider the possibilities offered by a third way of doing business – intermediation. Will the twenty-first century be the age of the cyber-broker?

CHAPTER 6 – DIGEST

What next?

Key message:
The nature of the business game is changing.

Why?

Because of three major trends:

- Globalisation
- Technological advance
- Uncertainty

and three major forces:

- individualism
- markets
- solidarity

What?

Globalisation means that traditional barriers, both business and cultural, are disappearing. Information technology has accelerated communication, trade and decision-making. And no one knows what will happen next.

We need to understand the forces at work. First, the individualism that encourages people to think for themselves, second, the markets that allow them to trade on their own account, and finally, the countervailing human impulse towards solidarity.

So what?

You need to understand that business can no longer be separated from politics or from social issues. You need to make your business more flexible.

CHAPTER 6

What next?

At the beginning of this book we talked about making the future your own. We referred to the imagination required, and the necessary determination to resist the pull of the mainstream. And we went on to sketch a framework that might enable you to achieve success by going against the flow. Without that framework, the future is the stuff of nightmares.

As we enter the twenty-first century, more and more companies are going to become used to the ideas of discontinuous change, invisible competitors and sudden changes to the rules of the game. This is not the law of the jungle – it's far more frightening than that. In the jungle, there is a hierarchy and there are rules: there are predators, there is prey, and one chases the other. The criteria for survival are more or less invariable – notably speed, strength and guile.

Now imagine a jungle where the graceful antelope becomes suddenly carnivorous and begins to prey on you, while the panther grazes peacefully in the fields and ant colonies join forces to become super-colonies in order to conquer and hold new territories. No game theory can help you here. Certainly not conventional game theory, which assumes that the nature of the game (what is winning and what is losing) is fixed, and that the rules are known and recognised by all competitors.

When the nature of the game is changing so radically, it is clearly no good trying to play by the old rules, analysing the history of your industry, assessing your competitors' likely moves, and trying to predict likely outcomes. Are we saying, then, that you should ignore past or current trends, choose your future and plough on towards it regardless? Certainly not.

Globalisation

One of the keys to survival in the twenty-first century is to be aware of the forces at work around you. The first and most obvious of these is globalisation. Although the word has become devalued through overuse, it nonetheless expresses a modern phenomenon that affects our daily lives, and is going to affect them ever more profoundly. Business networks are tightening as national tariff barriers are swept away and the trading blocs of Europe, North America and Asia/Pacific become increasingly dominant. Capital and goods are flowing ever more freely within this global market. This has had two main effects.

First, unprotected national economies have proved painfully vulnerable to market fluctuations, with a currency crisis in Thailand triggering a crisis of confidence throughout Asia, which in turn accelerated the disintegration of Russia and the collapse of investment in South America. Globalisation has reduced the tolerance of all but the best-run, most competitive economies. In the world of open markets, there is no escape for banks built on overextended borrowings, uncompetitive businesses or economies without sound monetary foundations.

Secondly, there is a worldwide blurring of boundaries as businesses spread their activities across numerous countries. In Europe, its most dramatic manifestation is the appearance of the euro, a common currency for the core members of the European Union. But this globalisation of business need not, as many people fear, lead to a merging of cultures. Indeed, the lesson of recent years is that if globalisation is to work we can't use a one-size-fits-all economic model. It must take account of different cultures, and there is no intrinsic reason why an ability to conduct business across borders should undermine national or regional cultures.

Information technology

The next inescapable force is information technology, which has accelerated a new kind of transparency in public and private life. That transparency is more marked in an established democracy like the United States, enabling the world to tune in to the Internet to read or hear about the US President's sexual habits. But even in China, where democracy has struggled to gain a foothold, the advent of satellite television and the growing accessibility of other electronic media are gradually making the social and political fabric more transparent.

Access to knowledge is the most significant driver towards social and political openness. If dictators and autocrats were able to control the output of information, they would be able to harness this technology to their advantage. But modern electronic media are far more difficult to control than printing presses and land-based television networks and telephone lines. And this growing access to knowledge is combined with a democratisation of economic power, in which it is possible to trade electronically anywhere in the world.

Technology-enabled transparency militates not only against repressive, secretive regimes, but against nation states. Language need not be a barrier, and, as the great issues of the day – the economy, environment and defence – become the subject of international debate, it becomes increasingly evident that they require co-ordinated international action.

Uncertainty

The rapid pace of globalisation, accelerated by technology, creates uncertainty – which in itself becomes a powerful force in shaping our world. As we peer anxiously into the future, uncertainty spreads across the picture like a smear of dirt or grease, obscuring our view. This frightens some people, particularly if they are fixated on the idea of trying to work out what is going to happen next. But theirs is the attitude of the mainstream thinker, the person who is happy only when the game is played as advertised, and everyone knows the rules. It might indeed be more comfortable if this were the case, but it isn't. The game is changing all the time, and so are the rules. If we have the courage to spurn the mainstream and travel against the flow, uncertainty need not frighten us.

If you can accept uncertainty as a fact of modern life, it can even be your ally. Other people, you must understand, are looking at the same smeared and smudged picture of the future. You may not know what is going to happen, but your competitors don't know either. And, if you have adopted a dynamic strategy that gives you the opportunity to create discontinuities, you may be better placed than anyone.

These, then, are the driving forces of today's business world. But they do not exist in isolation. They are complemented by sociopolitical forces that no enlightened business leader can ignore. Again, these are three-fold: individualism, securitisation and solidarity.

Individualism

The collapse of Soviet Communism at the end of the 1980s and the apparent triumph of Western capitalism helped to foster the cult of the individual. At a stroke, it seemed, the ideals and practices of socialism in all its many forms had become outdated and impractical. Throughout Europe, and in many other parts of the world, governments came under pressure to remove the 'dead hand of the state' from overprotected and inefficient industries. And, as privatisation became synonymous with progress and reform, political leaders began to question the rationale of state welfare systems that seemed to anchor large sections of the population in abject dependency. Self-help and self-reliance became the new watchwords, and they have yet to go out of fashion, more than a decade since the Thatcher/Reagan era which represented the apogee of capitalist triumphalism.

Business realities have compounded the sociopolitical trend towards the individual. Job insecurity has made people realise that they can no longer depend on their employer; the job-for-life culture so deeply rooted in Japan, other Asian countries, and to a lesser extent in Germany and France, is largely a thing of the past. As workers, we have adjusted, often painfully, to the demise of labour-intensive manufacturing industries, and the collapse of the communities associated with those industries. We have learned to become more self-sufficient, often working from home with the aid of personal computers, building up our own portfolios that will enable us to survive in our particular corner of the service industry that seems certain to dominate the twenty-first century.

As consumers, too, we demand ever-greater individual attention. We insist on greater choice in our home entertainment, choice we can exercise from our living-room sofa. We expect ever-higher levels of customisation in the things we buy. We try to look after ourselves with the help of personal trainers and therapists of many different kinds.

Markets

Closely related to individualism is the force that I call *securitisation*, by which I mean the way in which more and more products, companies, organisations, groups of people and even individuals are coming on to the market, so that they can be traded. 'Market forces' is the more familiar phrase, hence the subtitle used here. It used just to be companies, in which shares could be bought and sold on the stock market; then, with the removal of currency controls, it became currencies, and we remember how in the 1990s the activities of inspired gamblers like George Soros effectively decided the future of national economies. Now it is people. You may not be able to buy a piece of George Soros, but, if you buy shares in the American investment company Berkshire Hathaway, you are, in effect, buying a piece of Warren Buffett, the investment genius whose company it is.

Increasingly, we live in a world divided into two: the securitised and the unsecuritised. If you or your organisation can increase your financial liquidity by securitising, you do so. At the most basic level, we become individually securitised by taking out pensions or life insurance (while the insurance companies in which we invest spread their risk elsewhere round the global stock market). At the same time, many of us spread our risk by buying and selling on our own account. And so we join the ranks of the securitised – stakeholders in global capitalism. Almost anyone who makes enough money does it at the first opportunity: successful film stars start their own production companies; pop phenomena like the Spice Girls go into merchandising. Recently a growing number of football clubs in Europe and the US have gone public in an effort to diversify their ownership and achieve financial liquidity – and another part of our culture becomes securitised.

Meanwhile, there are many millions, not just the starving tribes of Africa, Mongolia and the Amazon jungles, who have no such stake, who are not securitised. These are ordinary people in Europe, the US, Asia, anywhere, who may work and pay rent but be unable to elevate themselves into the ranks of the securitised; or they may not work and may depend, to a greater or lesser extent, on state benefits. The gulf between the securitised and the unsecuritised, between rich and poor, is one of the most worrying and challenging features of the global economy.

Solidarity

In the Anglo-Saxon model so loudly championed by Milton Friedman and the Thatcherites/Reaganites, individuals and markets drive globalisation. But there is a countervailing force against the potentially destructive effect of unfettered global capitalism, and it is the human tendency towards solidarity. Since time immemorial, people have shown solidarity towards their families and communities. In more recent history, people have shown a broader solidarity with nation, class and tribe – and these loyalties have formed a vital part of the social fabric. At the dawn of the twenty-first century, this kind of solidarity is under threat: tribal loyalties, while they persist in less developed nations, are diluted by progress; the nation state, as we have seen, is in retreat; and, although class distinctions will persist in every society, developed countries have integrated more and more people into a huge, amorphous middle class, leaving working-class mass action a distant memory.

Despite all this, solidarity remains a powerful force. It bound the peoples of Russia and Eastern Europe together for most of the twentieth century, albeit via the stifling apparatus of the communist state. In Asia and central Europe, it is coming into its own once more, with a growing consensus that, although individual freedom is a vital ingredient in democracy, individualism and market forces cannot be allowed to run riot, for fear that we will lose the morality of caring for others upon which human society depends.

In Western Europe, the election of left-of-centre governments in nine of the eleven prospective members of the single currency signalled a change of heart. After years of free-market radicalism, and emphasis on privatisation and competition, in October 1998 the leaders of those nine countries, including Germany, France and Britain, signed up to a document called 'The New European Way', which talked of job creation and social and environmental responsibility. But 'The New European Way' is a long way from socialism on the Marxist model. It recognises globalisation, seeks to adjust to change, and 'combines a new economic dynamism with our well established and enduring commitment to solidarity, equal opportunities and social justice'.

Gradually, not only in Europe but around the world, the balance has shifted, as more and more people reach for forms of government and economic frameworks that offer more social underpinning. The Russian experience has probably been as chastening as any, as the world has witnessed the abject failure of the West's attempt to graft the standard Western model of capitalism on to a society without entrepreneurial values balanced by respect for property and the rule of law. The result has been gangster capitalism – a deeply disillusioning experiment.

Asian societies, which have evolved in many different ways, but for which the family has been the heart of business as well as social life, have found it almost equally difficult to cope with the demands of the free-market economy. And, as the Asian crisis promises a worldwide recession, even the free-market radicals have finally had to accept that they don't have all the answers.

In November 1998, *Time* magazine, no friend of socialism or even social democracy, carried a revealing article by Jim Rohwer discussing capital controls, anathema to any full-blooded free-marketeer. Rohwer studied Taiwan and concluded that capital controls could work after all.

The Taiwanese, he explained, had managed to modulate capital flows without interfering with free-market forces. They had limited turnover in the foreign-exchange market to between $150 million and $200 million a day, but they had not restricted the use of foreign currencies for trade in goods and services. Although the authorities had to be notified, foreign investors did not require permission to move capital or profits out of the country. Nor were the Taiwanese themselves restricted from investing abroad – except in China. Taiwanese citizens could send $5 million a year out of the country with no questions asked; a company could send out $50 million.

The Taiwanese had proved, said Rohwer, that capital controls could do what they were supposed to do: allow growth with stability. It seems inevitable that other Asian nations will follow Taiwan's example.

I mention these developments in world politics and economics not purely because they interest me, but because they affect the way we do business. We may not be able to predict what will happen next, but, if we are aware of the forces at work, we are less likely to be taken by surprise. It may be, for instance, that the Anglo-Saxon model for the world economy is in terminal decline, and that globalisation, instead of exporting the American Way, will gradually persuade Americans, whose ideology still springs from the individualism of the frontiersman, of the longer-lasting values of the Asian or European Way.

One thing that is clearly essential is that these different cultures should be reconciled. For cultures are now effective stakeholders in the global economy, and it is clear that one-size-fits-all capitalism is not the answer.

The twin pressures of globalisation and securitisation are forcing governments of whatever political persuasion to make more and more compromises with the forces of global capitalism. And astute capitalists, sensing their opportunity, are learning to negotiate with governments for bigger, longer-term contracts. That often means abandoning their long-held political convictions. The activities of Rupert Murdoch and News Corporation are particularly instructive here.

In 1993, Murdoch paid $525 million for a controlling interest in Star TV, Asia's biggest satellite broadcaster. William Shawcross, Murdoch's biographer, wrote in 1993:

It is hard to exaggerate the importance of Murdoch's acquisition of Star. The footprint of its satellites covers all Asia and the Middle East. Altogether there are three billion people under that footprint – about two-thirds of the world's population. It already has an audience of some 45 million people in 13 million homes across Asia. It already operates five channels – News, Sport, General Entertainment, Movies and a Chinese language channel. A sixth channel, in Hindi, is broadcast to India. Further channels are planned.

As Shawcross noted, Asian governments were never likely to greet this with total equanimity. Controlling or censoring newspapers is one thing. Controlling satellite broadcasts is extremely difficult. Hence Murdoch's charm offensive with the Chinese – which was to lead to his UK publishing company HarperCollins refusing to publish the memoirs of the former Hong Kong governor Chris Patten because they were thought too critical of China. Not that the courtship was all one way: the Vietnamese government in Hanoi persuaded Murdoch to fly from Peking to Hanoi to help advise them on restructuring Vietnamese television.

Rupert Murdoch's love affair with Asian communism has struck many observers as richly ironic. As Shawcross put it, 'One of the most assiduous salesmen of The Dream, a man who saw himself as an Agent of Influence for the American Way, was being asked in effect how to make communist-controlled television more popular.'

No less ironic was the fact that, while Murdoch was cuddling up to the Chinese, another super-capitalist, Bill Gates, was falling out with the US government. Stephen Houck, attorney for the US Justice Department, opened the largest antitrust trial since the IBM case of the 1970s in October 1998 by accusing Microsoft of 'throwing their weight around by using their ability to control Windows to intimidate their competition'. From the US government's point of view, one of the limitations on the power of any given business, any single entrepreneur, should be the competition. Hence its extreme sensitivity to the creation of cartels, or any deals or covert pressure that interferes with competition. For almost exactly the same reason, Britain's Monopolies and Mergers Commission (now known as the Competition Commission) was required to investigate Murdoch's bid for Manchester United on the grounds that, since he already owns the right to broadcast Premier League football in Britain, perhaps he should not also be allowed to own any club.

It is significant that, in these legal battles, it now appears to be the governments that are fighting the rearguard actions. The super-capitalists are the ones with the real power, and, although they may lose from time to time – as Murdoch did with Manchester United – the power shift is clear, and inexorable.

This, then, is the new global environment in which we operate – in which business people wield more real power than governments, but in which business, politics and diplomacy have an increasingly symbiotic relationship. Big business has always called the shots behind the scenes in the US, the campaign to bury Hillary Clinton's healthcare plan in 1993 being merely the most blatant recent reminder of the power of vested business interests. But the emergence of Russia's 'oligarchs', the business coalition led by Boris Berezovsky which funded President Yeltsin's 1996 re-election campaign and has been pulling the strings ever since, shows that this is no longer confined to Western capitalism.

We should not conclude from this that size is everything – that you have to be Bill Gates, Rupert Murdoch or Boris Berezovsky to exploit global information systems to the full. The David-and-Goliath story is retold over and over again in the modern world. We see it at the level of international politics and diplomacy, where, for all the United States' military might, rogue dictators like Saddam Hussein and Slobodan Milosevic can exploit divisions among members of Nato and the United Nations and pull the wool over their own people's eyes. And in a very different context we see it when a few dedicated members of Greenpeace force a multinational oil company like Shell to spend many millions of dollars on a fundamental change of policy.

Just as it behoves the giants to be aware of pressures from underneath, so it is wise for any aspiring business leader to appreciate the geopolitical forces at work – forces that could change the business environment overnight.

The opportunities for business

A large part of business consists of satisfying customers, or consumers. I mentioned consumer choice as one of the prime manifestations of individualism, and so it is; but it is changing, not least because consumers have discovered that it is possible to have too much choice. A world of endless choices can become both confusing and irritating. Where once it was a sign of class for a restaurant to have a long and comprehensive menu, now it is increasingly common, all over the world, to offer daily specials or limited-choice menus. Often, this is a sign that the food is freshly cooked rather than pre-packaged or bought in and defrosted in the microwave.

An even more bewildering set of choices faces customers in super-markets, with the result that a growing number of customers want to order electronically or by telephone – and supermarkets are setting up home-delivery services to cater for them. In other shops, customers face the kind of choices they are not qualified to consider. Do you want a stereo or pro-logic sound system with your new television? Do you want ABS brakes on your car? And as for your PC, do you want a whole lot of software systems you've never heard of? Many customers just want a quiet life. They want to be able to tell someone their requirements, explain their situation, then be supplied with the best possible product for their chosen purpose. They don't want a lot of superfluous, time-consuming choice.

Hence the opportunity for ambitious businesses to find new markets to satisfy. The spread of the Internet, mobile telephones and lighter and more powerful PCs is making electronic commerce a reality for more and more businesses and individuals, and bringing with it a still greater embarrassment of choices. Increasingly, busy people don't want information technology that only makes them busier. They expect suppliers of products and services to be able to satisfy their specific needs. With more demanding customers, the value proposition becomes more specific. Customisation is the order of the day – an area in which AT&T scored by reorganising into teams charged with understanding the needs of specific customer groups and delivering products, services and integrated solutions to meet those needs.

The Internet is a forum that cries out for a similar approach. There is an enormous amount of data on the Internet, but how to find the information we really need? There is an obvious opportunity here for libraries and other purveyors of information. More than that, I believe that the twenty-first century will see the emergence of a new generation of cyber-brokers, businesses that match goods and services to customers' requirements – earning commission by saving the customer time and therefore money.

Louise Kehoe, the *Financial Times*'s technology expert, calls them 'infomediaries', and cites as examples the stockbroking houses that have built Internet services in response to competition, and retail banks that offer on-line service to their customers. 'This new generation of middlemen ranges from electronic shopping agents that compare prices and product features to find the best deal for buyers, to information services that create special interest collections of electronic documents.' The crucial thing, as Kehoe notes, is that these intermediaries must add value. Good examples are the companies that harvest information from various electronic sources, then filter and repackage it to fit the needs of a particular industry segment, interest group, company or individual.

The market is changing. Already we can see businesses leaping traditional barriers in an effort to use the electronic media to reach more customers – with the first movers enjoying a crucial advantage. Inevitably, it seems, one of the companies best placed to exploit the new marketplace is Microsoft. Until recently a software company pure and simple, Microsoft is becoming an increasingly influential player in several other businesses.

Through its subsidiary Expedia, Microsoft is attacking the travel-reservations industry from two directions: on the one hand, it provides reservation services to consumers; on the other, it provides software for travel companies. Its key advantage is that, if a web customer uses Microsoft's Explorer browser, the first page he or she will see is Expedia. Although competitors pay Microsoft for favourable positioning, they may still be located a few screens away from Expedia.

Carpoint is Microsoft's attempt to use its position to enter another lucrative market, advertising used cars for sale. Microsoft charges car dealers around $1600 a month to list their inventories on its website, and so successful has it been that, despite General Motors' launch of its own GM Buypower website, Carpoint still has a more comprehensive list of GM used cars for sale.

Banking has also become a Microsoft target, the company having formed MSFDC, a joint venture with a payment processor that enables customers and service providers to receive money and pay bills over the

Web. No wonder various interests are challenging Microsoft in the courts.

Just as industry boundaries are blurring, so are national boundaries. The geographical spread of high technology is growing daily. Parts of the hi-tech industry are moving from Silicon Valley, California, to the silicon plains of Bangalore and other parts of India. France has just passed a law absolving IT specialists from having to meet normal visa requirements. If you are a hi-tech specialist, you are increasingly a citizen of the world.

In these circumstances, what can your business do to compete, to turn technology to its own advantage? These rapid changes may seem bewildering, but only if you are wedded to conventional wisdoms. Conventional wisdom, for instance, says that if you are a large company, you will never be capable of the kind of innovation that is to be found in dynamic young companies.

There is truth in this, of course, but it need not limit your ambition unduly. To be sure, there is little point in striving to foster innovation in the mainstream value chain of an organisation that is primarily aimed at running business as usual, through well-honed and efficient processes. Nor is it sensible for large, well-run organisations to acquire small, dynamic enterprises at prices that are often inflated. The rapid success of hi-tech companies like Amazon.com has misled certain people into thinking that the only way to compete is to grab the next Amazon.com before it becomes too big. In many cases, shareholders won't wear it anyway.

The answer is to take a different tack. Why not add to your mainstream business, in parallel, a venture-capital business? Hire and enable inno-vators to work independently, going against the flow, reporting direct to the CEO. Their brief should be to create something that does not undermine the core business, but significantly changes the rules of the game. Such businesses can be judged by four criteria: how far they change the rules, the extent to which they gain market acceptability, the extent to which they create new markets, and whether they can ensure at least one launch customer. It will not suffice to have a brilliant product or service if the market is not ready.

Once a venture-capital enterprise of this kind has proved its mettle, its leaders can entrust their enterprise to the core business to administer, while moving on to conquer new pastures. This enables innovation to live side by side with routine business management. It also costs much less than acquiring a thriving business, whose culture may easily clash with that of its new parent.

We can create our own futures, but only if we are prepared to defy the prevailing current, and go against the flow. Consider the mobile telephone. If the pioneers of this new technology had accepted the limits of the future as generally perceived, they might have thought of their products as appropriate only for emergency use, for cars, for outdoor events. They would never have believed that people would wander along the street making telephone calls, or use them on golf courses, or be obliged to submit to bans on their use in restaurants.

But Nokia, Ericsson, Orange, Motorola and others recognised an opportunity to create a new lifestyle, a new future, a discontinuity. It took courage, and a lot of chief executives would have missed out in similar circumstances. They would not have taken the risk of committing the necessary resources.

In 1996, Ericsson embarked on its largest-ever planning study, entitled '2005 – Ericsson entering the 21st Century'. Using academics, independent research organisations and consultants, the company examined not just its own industry of telecommunications, but the entire media industry. Ericsson was particularly aware of possible areas of convergence, as well as the increasing blurring of boundaries between component suppliers, suppliers of telecom equipment, and telecom operators. Three scenarios were developed. The first is called 'Service Mania', a world dominated by brokers, in which the content and service providers are the big financial winners. The second scenario, 'Gran Tradizione', envisages end-users, loyal to traditional operators, turning directly to content providers, with the result that traditional networks prosper. Finally, 'Up and Away – Full Speed Ahead' envisages a world in which the end-user gains access to advanced telecommunications systems virtually free of charge via the Futurenet, a broadband network capable of handling multimedia, video, TV and every kind of telephone. In this last scenario, many traditional operators will have disappeared from the market, leaving the manufacturers of terminals and other end-user devices to reap the industry's main rewards.

With these possibilities in mind, Ericsson identified ten critical issues that would enable the company to compete in any of the three scenarios. Just as crucially, the company identified a series of goals to satisfy customers, shareholders, employees and other stakeholders or potential stakeholders. It remains to be seen whether the company maintains its determination to create its own future, but the omens are good.

At KPMG, we do something similar with many of our clients. We extrapolate, not only from existing trends, but also from our own thinking, and create hypothetical newspaper front pages. 'Plastic China' – a hypothetical feature article – offers a vision of China that incorporates some imaginative guesses about global currency development and electronic payment methods. It is typical of our work in that it does not pretend to be a realistic assessment of the Asian financial world in 2005; rather, it aims to present a variety of high-probability futures.

The question is not whether the hypotheses we have outlined will actually come true. The question is how you would cope if they did come true – and they are sufficiently realistic that they could easily do so. If you would be utterly floored by such a hypothetical development, you may have reason to worry. Faced with these kinds of scenarios, many of our clients understand that the cost of doing nothing is likely to be so high that it simply ceases to be an option. Radical change is compulsory. At the very least, you should be asking yourselves: are we going against the flow, or have we allowed ourselves to be sucked into the mainstream?

The future is unknowable. The only thing that is certain is that if you drift with the flow that future will be limited.

Going against the flow is not a matter of defying nature. The salmon swims upstream in obedience to its survival instinct. It defies powerful currents, and obstacles of many kinds, but it remains absolutely in tune with its environment. We must be the same, aware of the forces that are shaping our world, but not slaves to the prevailing current, not distracted by the fads and fashions that are carried like flotsam in the mainstream.

The Fresh Horizons Story

How one company might learn to go against the flow

Episode 1

As chief executive of Fresh Horizons, Bill Colefax has made a good start. After twelve months in the job, he has forged an excellent working relationship with the current management team. Only yesterday the financial director mistakenly called him Clive – the name of the former chief executive – and went on to explain that this was easy to do because the transition from one chief executive to the next had been so seamless.

Fresh Horizons itself posted very respectable mid-term profits only a month ago, and has its fingers in many different pies in financial services. But Bill is getting restless. In particular, he is wondering if Fresh Horizons shouldn't get into the card business. He raises this at the board meeting.

Mike Fox is enthusiastic. He always is. As befits a former McKinsey man, he is unusually well informed about industry trends, and always interested in new ideas. The card business is just fantastic, says Mike. Did anyone know that they were using smart cards instead of traditional photo-passes at some of the smartest French ski resorts? Or that travelling on the underground would be revolutionised over the next few years in London, Paris and maybe even New York?

Soon, says Mike, we shall be in the era of the multifunctional, multichannelled card that serves as an identity card at work, carries your passport number, your bank account details, and can be inserted into your personal computer to allow you to make electronic cash transactions. The big question is: who will provide this card?

It won't be a bank, says Angie Scrivens in her dry, deadpan manner. Why not? comes the chorus. Because, says Angie, all the brightest ideas on card use in the past few years have come from retailers, supermarkets, and other new entrants to the market. That's because they are so much better at leveraging the customer relationship, says Trevor, the marketing director.

There's a brief silence in the board meeting. Then Gerald Leathwaite, the financial director, puts his oar in.

Listen, he says, there's no reason to get carried away with all this card business. Sure, there's plenty of mileage in it, and there are a lot of clever people out there doing clever things. But they won't all make money. There's nothing to stop us doing a deal with a card provider at a later date. In the meantime, we should concentrate on doing what we do best – namely, selling financial products.

For instance, says Gerald, there's plenty of growth in the mortgage business – particularly with our new young-family mortgage. And most of the insurance packages are going well. What we should be doing is bundling more of those products, so that people know that Fresh Horizons will take care of home, health, holidays, everything. That's the way to leverage the customer relationship.

Gerald's words prompt a murmur of approval, and perhaps relief, from about half the room. At the end of the meeting, there's no consensus, and Bill isn't at all sure about the way forward.

Episode 2

Bill has an idea. Why not get in touch with Liliane, his formidably clever friend who lectures at his old business school? It's at times like these that we all need a good guru.

Of course, says Liliane when Bill calls. And don't worry. You're not alone. These kinds of changes are taking place across any number of industries, and you need to think very carefully about the course you follow. They arrange to meet the following week.

Liliane has plenty to say. The first thing is that Bill is taking absolutely the right approach. These days, it's no good 'sticking to your knitting', as your financial director seems to want you to do. Before you know it, someone will come along and change the rules of the game so that you become irrelevant. In every corner of global business, boundaries are being crossed, or redefined. Customers are smarter and better informed. New market players are coming along from different industries, some-times, it seems, from nowhere!

Take telecommunications, for instance. Here is a thriving industry, accustomed to rapid change. But the impact of new technology has been such that telecommunications are now inseparable from electronics, computing and the media industries, like broadcasting. Deregulation and the application of common technological platforms are making so many things possible that no industry sector can regard itself as self-contained. Consider a company like British Gas. Once a gas supplier pure and simple, British Gas is increasingly involved in home security, insurance and credit cards. It even provides electricity, historically, its competitor fuel. But why not? Most businesses and households use both energy sources, so why shouldn't British Gas try to supply the lot? Anyway, electricity companies offer gas.

It's all too bewildering for some people – but that's because they think along tramlines. They have absorbed so much conventional wisdom over the years that they are prisoners of the prevailing current, pulled along by the mainstream. You've got to think for yourself, and be prepared to go against the flow.

Inspired by Liliane, Bill goes back to his board again and says: 'Look, we can't afford to sit back and wait to see what happens. I've had a look around and I've come to realise that our industry is just like many others in that it's undergoing deep structural change. If we stick to doing what we know best, we could suddenly find ourselves irrelevant. I'm not saying we've got to get into the card business, but we need to take a closer look at what's happening, and at what our customers are likely to want. What are they going to want to do with their money? What sort of things are they going to be prepared to pay for, and how will they want to pay them?

'We should look at behaviour. We should look at technology. We should look at processes, our own and other people's. Then we should start making decisions about what unique value we can provide, and where we should concentrate our main strategic effort. But right now I want to see everyone opening their minds and thinking.'

This time there's a palpable tension in the boardroom. People can sense that things are about to change. Some are excited, some uncomfortable. Mike Fox can hardly contain himself. Suddenly he's off into talking about the next stage after credit cards, when everyone has a personal organiser and a mobile phone, and when they start to buy and sell things electronically, by hand-held computer. So is the card business soon going to be obsolete? Gerald looks glum, and so do several people around him.

Episode 3

A few hours later, Bill knocks on the door of Gerald's office. 'You're not happy, are you?' he says.

'Well, no,' says Gerald. 'It's just that people in this business aren't all visionaries the way you might like them to be. A lot of them just like to do what they're good at, and go home at the end of the day, knowing that they've done their job and earned their money. If you turn everything upside down, you're asking for trouble. It'll be like it was when we moved office and installed the new computer systems – months of chaos before we went back to doing a lot of things the way we always had done them.'

'Come on,' says Bill. 'I never said I wanted to turn everything upside down. But you know as well as I do that we can't turn our backs on change. And I don't want us to follow everyone else. I want us to lead, to find some new way of satisfying our customers that is going to get us ahead of the competition. But I need your help, Gerald.' And Bill suggests that Gerald should come and meet Liliane.

When the three of them meet the following week, Liliane talks about the industry, about the new competition that has sprung up from supermarkets and telephone banking, and about the possibilities offered by the Internet, and Gerald begins to see that standing still is not an option. But then Liliane asks him what the obstacles are, and Gerald starts to list them: the fact that no one understands what the IT people are up to, that the company's structure makes it difficult for the marketing people to work alongside the product designers, and that the whole organisation is so overwhelmingly process-driven.

'But these same people and processes that you see as obstacles are actually your levers of change,' says Liliane. 'Start consulting these guys and bring them together. See what the marketing people really want and if the product designers can deliver it. Then get the IT people along too, and see if they have anything to offer. If you can't understand what they're saying and if they are not giving you value, you might think about outsourcing. Anyway, it sounds to me as if you need to rethink some of your processes.

'Remember, you need to try to turn your whole organisation to face the customer, and you need to get your executive team focused on delivering value for every stakeholder. But I guess the most urgent thing is to open up lines of communication.'

Gerald is silent for a while after the meeting, then he says to Bill: 'Well, you're the chief executive, so let's give it a go.'

Episode 4

At the next board meeting there is apparent unanimity about the need for a fresh look at strategy. Geena Bernstein, head of corporate affairs, says she will organise a special issue of the company magazine, to be delivered to every employee's home with a covering letter from the chief executive. The special issue will include contributions from several directors, and Liliane, Bill's favourite guru, has promised to write a provocative and entertaining article explaining the concept of trying to satisfy every one of the company's stakeholders.

Gerald, Angie and Trevor are to form working groups with representation from every part of the business. They will hold weekly meetings in different offices, trying to identify stakeholder value propositions, and report back to the board in three months' time with recommendations for action.

Within a few weeks, Bill Colefax realises there are several vital issues emerging. The first is that the IT department is almost a separate fiefdom. The IT director, Ivan Provalenko, has been clearly put out by the new approach, and his executives are not being at all helpful. Bill confides his worries to Gerald and Angie, and subsequently calls Ivan into his office. When Bill says he is going to invite two outside agencies to tender for the job of running the company's IT services, Ivan hands in his resignation.

Meanwhile, the working groups are coming up with various ideas. One is an extension of the employee share-ownership scheme, which is more widely supported than most of the management team had realised. Initial results from a customer survey suggest that the sales teams and 'financial advisers' have been plugging Fresh Horizons' products rather too assiduously; customers don't seem to take 'advice' seriously.

On the home-loans front, there is much animated discussion between marketing and product design. Under Trevor Phelps's leadership, a new product is being developed with the provisional title of 'home arranger'. The idea is that Fresh Horizons will offer its clients not only highly competitive mortgage deals, but will also undertake to take responsibility for the entire purchase, briefing solicitors, and even organising removal teams who will contact the customer.

At the next board meeting, Trevor proposes that the company's financial advisers be abolished. Some will have to be offered redundancy; others can be redeployed. 'People expect a certain level of financial advice whenever they contact us,' says Trevor. 'Our customers simply don't believe that our in-house financial advisers offer them any additional value. They would rather just have the best possible products, financial arrangements that make their lives simpler.' There is not a single dissenting voice.

Gerald, who has established a new rapport with the human-resources department, is busy developing a new set of measures to encourage and reward the kind of employee behaviour that can attract and retain loyal customers. It isn't easy.

Episode 5

A new atmosphere, almost a new culture, is beginning to take root within Fresh Horizons. The finance department under Gerald Leathwaite is now one of those most enthusiastically driving the change, and the whole management team is so highly motivated that Bill Colefax sometimes wishes he could control the flood of ideas.

There is one much bigger problem, however. The media have reacted with unexpected venom to the company's withdrawal of its financial advice service. 'FRESH HORIZONS OPTS FOR NEW FACELESSNESS' is only one of many derogatory headlines. A leading columnist has been spurred into a diatribe against organisations like Fresh Horizons that show 'complete contempt for the customer'. The PR fightback has come too late, and the company's share price has dropped 12 per cent in a week.

Geena Bernstein offers her resignation. But Bill won't accept. 'It's not your fault,' he says. 'It's everybody's. The fact is that we discussed the whole issue at the last board meeting, and it never occurred to any of us that this would be taken in the wrong way. After all, the only reason we decided to get rid of financial advisers was that the customers told us they didn't rate them.'

Geena is utterly distraught, and so are many of her colleagues. Her deputy, who was responsible for the press release on the day, has resigned, and will not be dissuaded. But, by the end of the week, Geena has been reassured, some of the prominent journalists have been persuaded to revise their attitudes, and the share price has made a slight recovery. But the whole company has been shaken.

At the next board meeting, there is some serious soul-searching. Bill, who has discussed the whole crisis at length with Liliane, summarises the situation. 'We're all to blame,' he says. 'And no one more than me. We forgot two of our key stakeholders. We were so obsessed with giving the customers what they wanted, and squaring our own employees in the process, that we forgot about the regulators – the media and the public in this case – and we failed to explain the situation adequately to our shareholders. In the past few weeks I've thought about resigning myself, but I rejected the idea, and I'm so glad we've dissuaded Geena. We're bound to make mistakes when we're driving change the way we are; we've just got to learn from them. We must think about all our stake-holders all the time, and one of the best ways of doing that is to try to achieve some long-term redefinition of those relationships.

'To that end, I'm pursuing the possibility of an alliance with one of the leading credit-card companies. It's having access to different markets via different technologies that matters. If we can't make the connections, we will simply miss all the best deals. We must have global reach.'

Episode 6

A year later, what has changed at Fresh Horizons? The outsourcing of IT has worked better than many expected, chiefly because, in Zorro Solutions, the company found the right partner. The contact was sufficiently flexible to allow for new systems to be introduced as the business's priorities changed, and Zorro's reward was linked to Fresh Horizons' achievement of its business aims, along with the performance of its share price – which has climbed steadily since the fiasco over the financial advisers.

The company's home-loans business is growing rapidly, and Fresh Horizons is widely admired for the way it makes life easier for home buyers. Marketing becomes easy when the media are on your side, giving you free publicity.

The alliance with Mastercard also looks like being successful, with new customers springing up all over Europe, where Fresh Horizons is well ahead of the game on home-loans, and competing well on the insurance front as well.

Mike Fox has been put in charge of business development, with mixed success. A scheme to float off a travel agency as a subsidiary on the back of existing travel-insurance business ended in failure. More than thirty shops were opened in the south of England and the north of France, but within six months they had been bought at a knock-down price by a consortium of ferry operators and the Virgin group, who were always far better placed to deliver customer value by getting them from A to B. They managed to freeze out Fresh Horizons, which sustained a loss of £2 million on the entire venture.

But another subsidiary has proved much more successful. This was a new car-insurance business, developed in partnership with Philips, providing car insurance linked with the very latest in-car navigation systems. With the aid of an in-car computer that can be synchronised with almost any mobile phone, drivers can communicate with FHP CarSure operators, who can perform any number of tasks on their behalf: while drivers keep their hands on the steering wheel, FHP CarSure will check traffic conditions, provide information about hotels in the vicinity, make bookings for meals, flights or even concerts, send faxes and e-mails to offices. FHP CarSure is widely regarded as the leader in its field – making the motorist's life easier.

In several areas – notably home loans and car insurance – Fresh Horizons can be said to have changed the rules of the game. At the dawn of the twenty-first century, it is an admired company, with turnover and share price on a healthy upward curve. As a reminder of what might have happened had the company not decided to go against the flow, its great rival Commerce Bank has found its share of the market declining and ended up being taken over by HSBC.

PART TWO

Some Practical Guidance

CHAPTER 7

Managing people against the flow

Once you have decided to go against the flow, your fitness for purpose becomes the crucial issue. In this chapter, we examine how you can best ensure that your people are aligned with your strategy. This is one of the most difficult tasks in management, requiring every bit as much seriousness and commitment as any other. The temptation is to assume that strategic issues are the ones that require all the intellectual fire-power, and that human resources is simply the 'touchy-feely' stuff that can be delegated to a suitably sympathetic senior person within your organisation. Wrong. If anything, the people issue is the most challenging of all, throwing up a formidable series of obstacles that are intellectual, political and emotional, often all at once.

So many organisations assume that, once the new vision has been articulated, the people within have what it takes to make it happen – with the help, perhaps, of some slight tinkering with the organisational structure. The reality is that changing the strategy without realigning behaviour, skills and knowledge, is futile. A new strategy can be likened to your organisation's wishbone. But people are the backbone, without which you can do nothing.

And yet how often have we seen organisations attempt to operate with a wishbone in place of a backbone? Glaring examples of this kind of

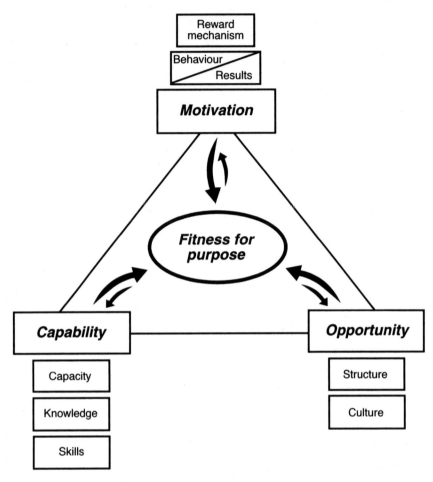

Changing behavoiur: the virtuous triangle

misconceived behaviour are to be found among Europe's privatised
industries. Even a decade after privatisation, most attempts to persuade
the people working in European electricity, water, gas and railways to
embrace the concept of client service have barely got off the ground.
Usually, it is because the organisation – massive, overstaffed, ossified by
years of dictatorial control and rigid hierarchies – still retains a culture
built around systems and procedures. The customer has to fit in with the
system, rather than vice versa. No flexibility, let alone any degree of

customisation, has been allowed for within the system; and the behaviour of the customer-facing personnel is tailored to the system. The same is true of many large retail organisations, particularly banks, insurance companies and airlines.

There will always be a conflict between system and customer focus, particularly in large organisations. Efficient systems lower transaction costs and enable an organisation to employ lower-skilled individuals to deal with the customer. Customer focus, on the other hand, requires flexibility – the ability to change the system, in other words – a willingness to customise a product or service, and the empowerment of highly skilled staff.

This chapter is written on the assumption that your organisation has adopted a vision and strategy that will require your people to do different things, or at the very least to do things differently. The challenge we face, therefore, is not to reinvent the theories of human-resource management but something more specific: how are we going to alter people's behaviour – not temporarily but permanently – so that they share a commitment to put the business's new strategy into practice every day?

To address this question, we must return to the concept of fitness for purpose introduced in Chapter 3. When we considered people under this heading, we were concerned with capability, motivation and opportunity – the three corners of a triangle. A virtuous triangle, you might say. Why should circles have a monopoly of virtue? Let's deal first with capability, which is essentially a combination of skills and knowledge.

Capability

Almost certainly, we shall need to improve both skills and knowledge. Knowledge, of course, can be gained from books, or via the classroom, or downloaded from electronic formats. Skill, on the other hand, requires experience, training and coaching. It requires an element of trial and error. Whereas, for instance, you can learn history in a classroom and by reading, you cannot become an airline pilot by the same means – even though much of the work of a modern pilot consists of mastering skills that have been codified into checklists and procedures. There is still no substitute for practical experience – the situational awareness that a pilot, for instance, develops from experience.

One of our own clients, whose confidentiality we must protect, provides a real-life example. This was a bank which bravely decided to change the rules of the game for its corporate clients. Instead of waiting for the clients to ask for off-the-shelf products, the bank decided to create 'solutions' – bundled products and services aimed squarely at the issues faced by these particular clients. The idea was sound enough: by customising its products and services, the bank promised greater value for its clients, differentiating the bank and enabling it to charge a premium. To execute this new strategy, the bank put together training courses for its salespeople. When they took their new products to market, however, the sales staff found it impossible to sell the new offerings. They complained that the new packages were too complicated and the customers didn't want them. Couldn't the bank go back to business as usual? they asked.

This left the bank with three options:

- Admit they had been too ambitious and back down
- Dismiss the complaints as self-indulgent, and keep the pressure on
- Identify the true source of the problem and address it

Happily, the bank chose the last of these options. After a preliminary investigation, it was established that the problem was not strictly to do with training, but with culture. The bank's salespeople, overwhelmingly male, shared a macho culture in which they aspired to a lone-hero ideal. Making a sale was seen as the equivalent of scoring a goal, or perhaps more like a fighter pilot notching up a 'kill'. The client, if not actually scorned, was seen as a passive victim whom it might be necessary to hoodwink in order to make a sale. As for their own organisation, the sales staff tended to characterise many of the people around them as pen-pushers and bureaucrats, obstacles rather than colleagues. In their eyes, the only way anything really got done was if one of them went off and did it by himself. Not surprisingly, there was little or no co-operation between departments.

In stark contrast with this prevailing culture, the bank's new strategy required the following kinds of behaviour:

- teamwork
- research and planning
- understanding of the client's business, and not just the bank's products
- willingness to be coached by others and compare reactions

This was clearly a case of culture shock. How to change such entrenched attitudes? Above all, how to embed a cultural change into the reward mechanisms? This was a major challenge.

The bank's reward mechanism did not recognise, let alone reward, results achieved by a team or group. Mentoring or coaching were alien concepts. To ask for help was perceived as a sign of weakness, not of open-mindedness and professionalism. Planning and research were anathema to the gung-ho, let's-just-do-it culture.

The problem may seem a clear one, but the solution was – and is – by no means simple. In this case there were two or three – and there usually are at least that many – possible alternatives. Should you, for instance, institute a culture change without delay, making it clear to every member of your sales force that they must learn to be open-minded, collegiate and sensitive, or get out? Or should you accept that, for better or worse, this is the sales force you have, and that it would be foolish to try to change the leopard's spots? Or should you try something in between, trying to influence those you consider open to new ideas, tolerating the incorrigible, and changing your reward, recruitment and promotion policies so that you attract more of the salespeople you want in the future?

I mention this case study primarily to illustrate the point that raising an organisation's capability is about more than just training and education. It may, as we have seen, require fundamental re-engineering of the company's entire system of measurements and rewards – which leads me on to the subject of motivation.

Motivation

Obviously, people without the necessary capability are unlikely to be motivated for long, so that is the first essential. But motivation, the second corner of our virtuous triangle, is no less indispensable. Even when your staff have acquired the necessary skills and knowledge, they will almost certainly need help before they have the will to do new things, or to do things differently.

Experience has taught me that where people are concerned you don't get what you can't measure. If you want to improve your chances of persuading people to behave in a particular way, you should begin by measuring what they achieve by their current behaviour. Your more difficult task, then, is to measure what they can achieve by the new kinds of behaviour you wish to promote. You need to identify behavioural elements that are (a) measurable and (b) directly linked to desired results. Performance measurement needs to become two-dimensional.

Achievement criteria

• Client enthusiasm
• Project management
• Professional skills

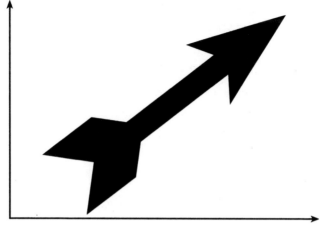

Behaviour criteria

• Team working/transcending boundaries
• Focus on results
• Quest for excellence
• People care and fun

Performance comprises achievement and behaviour

Once we can define behaviour-adjusted performance, we can create the essential steps in a reward mechanism that motivates people to adopt behaviour that will increase performance. In Chapter 3 we gave an example with market traders and risk-adjusted results.

Returning to our bank example, we have to find a way of measuring teamwork and preparation as an index by which we can adjust sales; then we can reward our salespeople according to genuinely behaviour-adjusted results. This mechanism in place, there is one further step to take if we want to embed the ideas of learning and open-mindedness: we should reward people for taking coaching courses, or for passing on their knowledge and skills to others. This might seem a laborious process in a business where the strategy is more or less understood, subject only to incremental changes; but, when you are creating discontinuities, it is absolutely essential. When managing people against the flow, you can't afford to let members of your team be sucked back into the mainstream. It is one of the factors that make it so much easier for new entrants to a market. When you are dealing with an organisation that is used to travelling in the mainstream, it is almost inevitable that, when you make a sudden change of direction, you will leave some behind.

Opportunity

We now come to the third and final corner of our virtuous triangle. Once someone has the requisite capability and mobility, it remains only to put that person in an appropriate job. The extent to which an organisation can play the intermediary role, linking capability, motivation and opportunity for each member of staff, will determine its own ability to change the rules of the game and make the competition irrelevant. But there are various obstacles in the way of opportunity, and the biggest by far is an organisation's structure.

Most organisation structures contain certain kinds of silos that oblige people to stick to a particular line of work. Even in advertising agencies, where the culture promotes job flexibility, it is rare for a project manager to move into design or to take on a client-facing role. Then there are hierarchies, levels of seniority that make it difficult to move someone without upsetting someone else. And of course there are networks, formal or informal, in which certain people are favoured while others are effectively frozen out. A certain amount of favouritism is an inevitable result of human nature, but every effort should be made to dismantle the kind of constellations of power in which directors or executives are like barons, who effectively own a certain number of opportunities, and farm them out among their own supporters, the better to bolster their own positions. It goes without saying that there will be more of these barriers in established companies than in newer, nimbler ones.

Modern high-technology companies have many fewer problems in this area, with many of their specialists able to operate very much in their own way, keeping their own hours while keeping in touch electronically – as Debra Engel, senior vice-president of corporate services at 3Com, the California-based computer-networking business, explained in an interview with the *Financial Times* in July 1998. 'We have moved on,' she said, 'from paternalistic organisations where people at the top had all the answers, to those where the relationship with employees is collaborative and sharing, more of a partnership.'

At 3Com, people are free to choose their own terms of employment. They work flexible hours, are entitled to flexible pensions and enjoy benefits packages that do not recognise status. Staff are encouraged to make their work fit in with their personal lives so that they enjoy the maximum fulfilment – and are not tempted to go off and work for a competitor. Adjustment to the new ways of working has been hardest for management, according to Debra Engel. Whereas personal calls and Internet use via the office used to be monitored and discouraged, now these are regarded as benefits of working for 3Com. Old notions of hierarchy are being so enthusiastically cast aside that a new leadership programme was introduced for directors and vice-presidents, encouraging them to 'sit in community' with no chairman and no fixed agenda, so that they discuss their affairs in the most open-minded fashion.

If 3Com can complete the virtuous triangle in this way, it is confident it can hold on to its best people even though a competitor may be offering a better-paid job – because life at 3Com is so congenial that to move would involve unacceptable switching costs.

It is entirely possible, of course, that you will discover that, with your current personnel and organisational structure, you simply won't be able to complete the triangle. In which case, your fitness for purpose having fallen short of the ideal, you will have no choice but to reduce your ambition. This need not be an admission of defeat.

CHAPTER 8

Financial control against the flow

The measurement principle

It would be impossible to run a business without financial control. Why? Because financial controls deal with the results of actions taken by the people who are trying to execute your chosen strategy. The bottom line is a vital measurement of a business's success or failure, and there is a basic but often forgotten principle of business life: you get only what you measure.

When you choose to go against the flow, there are vital implications for financial control, which should be able to tell you whether your new strategy is working. But everything depends on what we measure. Do we measure only the results of our actions? Or can we also measure the actions – or behaviour – that led to this particular result?

Most people would say that you should measure both. But how? In most organisations today, behavioural measurements are the responsibility of business managers, while financial measurements are left in the hands of the financial controllers. But does it really make sense to have one set of people measuring results, while another set of people, differently trained, with different perceptions, measure the behaviour that produces the results?

Typically, what happens is this. The financial controller decides which measures are necessary to ensure the financial wellbeing of the organisation. But he or she has little or no understanding of the behaviour required by business managers – even though such behaviour is supposed to be geared towards the consistent, effective and efficient achievement of those results. It is axiomatic that behaviour is bound to have an effect on results, and yet there is an organisational hiatus where there should be a connection. Consequently, there can be no certain coherence between what the company measures and what it does. You could easily be measuring the wrong things.

Let us take a hypothetical example: a company in the document-management business. In a meeting between the chief executive and the business managers it is agreed that the previous corporate strategy, which has been simply to sell equipment, is no longer in line with the business of document management. The company decides, therefore, that over the next two years it will ask its top salesmen to get to know their clients' businesses in much greater depth, to produce proper client development plans, to design and propose total document-management solutions, and even try to win outsourcing contracts.

Meanwhile, no one in the organisation is aware that a financial measure relating to the cost of sales (which includes time spent by the sales force in preparing to go to market) is about to create serious problems in the implementation of this new strategy. The measure is left in place. Over the next few months, as the top salesmen work with the technical teams to establish better long-term relationships with clients, they begin to receive memos from business managers and financial controllers that costs of sales are becoming unacceptably high. Sales teams are instructed to bring the costs of sales back to previously acceptable levels. Not surprisingly, the sales force becomes exceedingly frustrated by these contradictory demands. The company's best salespeople resign, and there is a consequent reduction in overall sales.

Eighteen months later, consultants are asked to intervene. The consultants point out that the new strategy was always going to require an initial period of investment, during which the initial cost of sales was bound to rise; over the longer term, however, as bigger contracts were secured, these costs as a proportion of sales would diminish, and overall profitability would improve. The financial measures are adjusted accordingly – but the costs over eighteen months have been high.

This example illustrates how easily a single, straightforward and long-accepted measure can create a major obstacle to the implementation of a new strategy.

It is vital, therefore, that, if you choose to go against the flow, you should gather top executives, financial directors and business managers together and ensure that everyone understands that a major strategic shift demands a complete review of financial measures. Without such a review, you will never be able to ensure consistency between results and the actions that lead to those results.

The airmanship principle

Aeroplane pilots are not mere plane drivers. They are required to display good airmanship, which consists of doing a number of things in a particular sequence. The ANC (Aviate, Navigate, Communicate) principle also happens to illustrate what we need to do in creating consistency between financial controls and business strategy. All aspiring pilots are taught from Day 1 that, whatever the situation in which they find themselves, they must apply the ANC principle in its correct order.

Aviate. Keep the plane flying in controllable fashion. What this means in financial terms is that you have to keep the company solvent in terms of working capital and cash flow. The alternative is to condemn the business to bankruptcy, which is the equivalent of crashing the plane. This is why most financial directors have devised what might be termed solvency dashboards that contain the key financial measures – whether in monetary amounts or ratios – that help them 'aviate' their organisations. Of course, they don't always work. Now and then, businesses go bankrupt, just as planes crash – albeit rather less often. We shall return to this point later in this chapter.

Navigate. This deals with direction and altitude. The pilot needs to know whether he is going in the planned direction; if he is not, he needs to know where he is and how to get back on course. Timing is also important: he can't afford to run out of fuel. And, of course, the pilot must ensure that he is flying at the right height to avoid hills, mountains and buildings, especially in the approach to landing.

For the financial controller, this means having a 'navigate' dashboard with the appropriate financial measures that enable the organisation to check that it is implementing its planned strategy; if it is not, he needs to know what he should do to get back on course without running out of resources, in order to reap the rewards of the strategy – the equivalent of making a safe landing. Unfortunately, most financial directors do not have a 'navigate' dashboard at their disposal. Their nearest instrument is probably the budget, with its twelve-month time horizon, subject to revisions every three months or so. This is by no means an adequate substitute.

Communicate. Most budgeting processes are aimed at cost containment. Little attention is paid to revenue beyond the most rudimentary estimates, varying from 'Let's be realistic, guys' – which means we'll go by last year's figures, give or take 5 per cent – to 'Let's go for the stars', meaning let's be as bullish as possible, given that we have no real direction, altitude, weather conditions, clearance to land and so on. As every pilot understands, only the air-traffic controllers have the full picture of what is happening in the airspace under their control, so they are uniquely placed to regulate the flow of air traffic and take responsibility for avoiding aircraft collisions.

In the same way, business leaders and financial controllers must establish reliable lines of communication, so that the organisation has complete situational awareness, and what is planned corresponds with what is done and what is measured. This requires going beyond the traditional budget-control meetings where business leaders merely attempt to justify why they are where they are. If we are to go against the flow, we have to have the fullest possible communication. That way, like pilots and their air-traffic controllers, we have a good chance of avoiding that potentially destructive collision between measures and behaviour.

But how do we integrate financial measures into the business strategy? The answer is we don't – because we must not allow this question to arise. Financial measures ought to form an integral part of the business strategy from the beginning. In other words, as soon as we identify a strategic initiative, we need to ask ourselves two basic questions:

- What are the desired results and how can we measure them?
- What are the main behavioural drivers and how do we make sure that the measures we have chosen do not constrain them but encourage and support their attainment?

If these two questions can be answered satisfactorily we should achieve 'behaviour-adjusted' performance – achieving the desired objectives by adopting the appropriate behaviour and actions.

If we go back to the example of the document-managing company mentioned a few pages ago, we have two choices during the investment period: either we drop cost of sales as a key measure and focus on total sales per account and contract extension, or we continue to monitor cost of sale but with a high ceiling in order not to constrain the desired behaviour from the salesforce. While this approach stops day-to-day financial dashboards from inhibiting strategy implementation, it does not really enable the strategy. In other words, using the airmanship principle, this deals with 'aviate' but not with 'navigate'.

Let's take another example: a British retail bank which decided to use department stores and supermarkets as branch-management best practice, and consequently implemented financial measures aimed at comparing revenue per square foot and per head. At the same time, the head office decided to implement an important strategy aimed at improving client profitability, to ensure that each branch would analyse its portfolio of clients and determine which were the most likely to buy more products and services from the bank.

These two sets of measures – top-line per-unit cost (square foot and head count) on the one hand and profitability on the other – led to a great deal of confusion among the branch managers, which in turn led to erratic behaviour. The bank failed to achieve both objectives and was forced to close down a number of branches in the name of rationalisation.

What lesson can we learn from this example? The financial director of the bank failed to translate the bank's strategy into an appropriate dashboard. The fundamental questions he should have asked himself were: Which is the driver and which is the result? Would top-line per-unit cost lead to better client profitability, or the reverse?

The answer, clearly, is that focus on better client profitability would have led to better client focus on the part of the branches, whose staff would have been retrained in the way they sold to clients, understanding the products more fully and making better use of customer information. In other words, they would have created a customer-centric culture with the administrative workload being shifted towards the corporate back office through the use of IT. The result would have been improved top-line per-unit cost and not the reverse!

The objective of this chapter, like each of the three chapters in Part Two, is not to be an exhaustive treatise on the subject but simply to flag a number of implementation issues that could, if not properly addressed, be a significant impediment to success.

Above all, a radical business strategy requires a fundamental rethink of the key financial measures according to the fundamental principle that 'You get what you measure'. This means, of course, that the wrong measures can lead to the wrong behaviour. It is essential, therefore, to link results, measures and behaviours in order to achieve behaviour-adjusted performance.

CHAPTER 9

Using information technology against the flow

If you aspire to lead your business against the flow, you cannot possibly ignore the influence of information technology. On the other hand, you do not want to be blinded by science. In this short chapter I propose to highlight, in non-technical language, the two issues that are most likely to affect your business strategy. Singly or collectively, and sometimes in unfamiliar guises, these are the issues that figure most often on the CEO's agenda.

- The application of packaged computer systems known as ERPS (Enterprise Resource Planning Systems), such as SAP, BAAN, Peoplesoft, JD Edwards etc. Few business managers or technicians fully appreciate the profound influence these systems can have on your entire business.
- The familiar question of whether IT can genuinely help you achieve sustainable competitive advantage. Much has been written on this subject, but very few convincing conclusions have been reached.

Every day these issues are being tackled with huge allocations of money but only the sketchiest understanding of the implications. The growth rate of the leading ERP suppliers and the number of companies that have decided to adopt these packages is eloquent testimony to their popularity and importance. Between 1994 and 1998 the sales revenues of Oracle's ERP systems rocketed from $2 billion to over $7 billion, while the revenues of the German SAP increased even faster, from $1 billion to almost exactly $5 billion. The sums involved mean these decisions can be taken only at the highest levels. But are the decision makers fully informed when they endorse these huge expenditures? Often, they are not.

In much the same way, IT strategy finds its way on to the CEO's agenda in the guise of knowledge management, electronic commerce or intranets. Business literature abounds with examples of how the Internet, data warehousing or some other creative use of IT has transformed the running of a business. But are these substantial investments matched by an appreciation of the low barriers to imitation and the rapid erosion of competitive advantage that often results? Only rarely.

Let me deal first with what I call the ERP Trap.

The ERP Trap

In the pre-ERP world, companies developed separate systems to regulate different functions such as manufacturing, finance or human resources. The linkages between these systems were in most cases extremely complex and ponderous. Gradually, this lack of connectivity – exacerbated by poor documentation and a plethora of programming languages and incompatible hardware – created mounting frustration among the business community. Little wonder, then, that when ERP packages appeared, offering well-documented and highly integrated systems, business managers were eager customers. Suddenly, it seemed, they had the opportunity to solve all their problems at once, while simultaneously acquiring a tool with which they could standardise key measures and reports, and thereby control umpteen different operating entities, spread right across the globe.

So far, so good. ERP systems, despite their costs, have proved that they can add value to a business. There is a price to pay, however, which goes beyond the investment required to buy and implement these packages. ERPs can solve yesterday's problems, but in a subtle and insidious way, they can all too easily create a whole new range of problems of their own.

AgrEvo, a German agrochemicals group, is a case in point. In August 1998, company executives complained to the *Financial Times* that the SAP System they had installed at the beginning of the year had generated a host of new administrative tasks and made them uncomfortably dependent on highly paid ERP specialists. 'Ten years ago,' said Stephen Braund, head of UK operations and project leader, 'the skill sets this company valued most were in chemistry. It is rapidly getting to the point where IT is gaining the upper hand. That is a worry. IT is critical but it is not a core competence.' Braund's advice to others was not to be seduced by the technology: 'Stick to what you know and what you need the system to achieve. Then make sure the technical guys deliver it.'

But the chief executive who wants to make IT an integral part of a new strategy must go a little further, venturing into areas that are often carefully guarded by those with specialist technical knowledge. Please bear with me. I do not propose to start getting technical. On the contrary, I believe that there are fundamental issues at stake here that are best expressed in simple terms.

A packaged system is a model of an organisation or part thereof. Like all models, it is based on a number of assumptions as to how the organisation should perform its various functions. These assumptions break down into two categories: the fundamental and the specific. First, the fundamental assumptions – so fundamental in many cases that even the designers of the system are not aware that they are making them.

Take, for example, a purchasing system aimed at a food manufacturer. A designer will probably assume that a manufacturer will buy raw materials and packaging materials from suppliers. As a result, the designer will design a system that recognises the concept of a supplier, a price list and a discounting mechanism. However, should the food manufacturer decide (which is often the case) to buy his commodities, such as sugar and cocoa, in the worldwide market, he will find himself requiring, over and above a supplier-driven system, a trading system. Instantly, the concept of a price list is rendered meaningless – the price in this instance being determined by global supply and demand, which may vary daily or even hourly. Discount mechanisms, when they exist, may be applicable where supply exceeds demand but cease to be applicable in the reverse situation.

And as for the supplier, he scarcely exists either. Since the entity supplying the physical commodity is likely to be different from the broker doing the deal, the supplier is, in effect, virtual. It may even become necessary to take a bet about future prices and buy commodity futures options which are very remote from the physical goods. Clearly, this kind of activity must be managed quite differently from the usual supplier-driven purchasing function. More crucially, if this activity represents a significant part of the total purchasing bill, then the ERP system orginally chosen will no longer match the needs of the manu-facturer.

The second category of assumptions is specific, explicit, and usually quantitative. Every business deal is conducted according to certain assumptions – typically, the purchase of a certain number of products and categories, within a range of prices that allows for discounts in particular circumstances. These assumptions are often called parameters. They do not in any way alter the fundamental assumptions but they give a certain amount of leeway to the user to vary terms of business. Such parametric tables are often fallaciously presented to the user as 'the way to customise your system to your needs'. I say fallaciously because the level of customisation is at the margin, while the basic model of how the business is conducted remains the same. So long as the enterprise does not alter the way it does business in any fundamental way, the ERP system will add value and support the business through better and standardised timely information for the organisation. However, since we are dealing with organisations that may decide to change their basic strategy and go against the flow, it is clear that sooner or later they are going to need to run their businesses in a way that conflicts with the fundamental assumptions embedded in the ERP system.

In such a case, the question arises as to which logic should dominate. Should it be the logic of the system (bearing in mind that to change the system would require a huge adjustment in terms of time and money), or should it be the business logic that requires changing the rules of the game in order to make the competition irrelevant? In circumstances such as these, we find that the ERP system that so neatly solved the problems of yesterday has created a series of obstacles to the future development of the business. In essence, the ERP system is constraining the enterprise into a rigid model of how business is to be done!

The worrying possibility arises that, just as yesterday's business leaders left a legacy of badly designed, unconnected systems, so today's leaders might be mortgaging the future by preparing a legacy of strategy-limiting, or even strategy-destroying, systems for tomorrow's leaders. So does this mean that ERP systems are bad for your health?

Absolutely not! Business leaders must stop relying on purely technical advice; they must separate their businesses into non-core activities on the one hand and strategically important areas on the other. Then, and only then, can they creatively adopt the rigidities built into the ERP systems for the non-core activities and find other solutions for those business areas that are likely to be pivotal to their future strategy.

In an important article in the *Sloan Management Review* in 1994, N. Venkatraman divided IT-enabled business transformation into five levels. The two most basic levels, which Venkatraman defines as 'evolutionary', are 'localised exploitation' and 'internal integration' – in other words, the redesigning of specific processes to improve internal organisation. Within this relatively narrow context ERP systems can be of clear benefit. The three higher levels, which Venkatraman defines as 'revolutionary', are, in ascending order, 'business process redesign', 'business network redesign' and 'business scope redefinition'. Any business that aspires to go against the flow must aim at these higher levels and be prepared to redefine its scope. And at these levels, for the reasons I have given, it is bound to be extremely difficult for an ERP system to be sufficiently flexible.

What of the future of ERP systems?

The lack of flexibility in today's ERP systems derives from the way they were constructed. In simple terms, today's systems are written in programming languages that are reliable because they are based on particular business models. Adherence to these models makes radical change complex, expensive and sometimes downright dangerous. So what is the answer? The answer, I believe, lies in another type of programming language which exists today and is known in the trade as object-oriented language. This type of software is specifically designed to make change easy, quick and cheap. If we had access to object-oriented ERP systems, we would go a long way towards solving the problems I have just outlined. So what, you might well ask, is the problem? Why don't ERP suppliers build more object-oriented systems? My guess is that there are two reasons.

First, there does not exist a single globally adopted standard for object-oriented languages. Consequently, current or would-be suppliers are afraid to take the first step and find that a standard other than the one they have adopted wins the day. Secondly, they have invested heavily in existing technology and wish to keep it in the marketplace for as long as their clients will tolerate it before reinvesting in new technology.

Our awareness of this problem should exert pressure on suppliers to make the jump and provide us with software that does not restrict our strategic options.

IT and sustainable competitive advantage

A second issue of vital importance to business leaders is the ability of IT to confer on the enterprise a distinct competitive advantage that it can sustain for long enough to enable it to differentiate itself from its competitors and thereby gain market share and improved profitability. Clearly, the creative use of technology can create an advantage for a company. We only have to think of Amazon's use of the Internet as a distribution channel to sell books direct to the consumer; or the way that Walmart, Marks & Spencer, Virgin and many others have used data mining to establish customers' buying patterns and target them with other products. The more important issue, however, goes beyond using IT for competitive advantage. It revolves around sustainability. Once we have achieved differentiation, how can we keep the barrier to imitation high enough to prevent competitors from merely adopting the same technological platform and thereby eroding the advantage we worked so hard to gain?

In the short term, there is a significant barrier that enables the first mover to gain an advantage without worrying about competitors. This is what I call intellectual inertia – the fact that most competitors will initially tend to go into denial mode and discount the new application as merely a 'blip', here today, gone tomorrow. If the phenomenon persists, those same competitors move into the 'why we are not in the same game' phase, offering multiple reasons that enable them to rationalise their own inaction. For intellectual inertia, you need only look once again at those retail banks that have been watching department stores, supermarket chains and even airlines steal customers from them and continue to do so. The mindset in these institutions remains intent on inaction in this field for reasons that essentially come down to denial and rationalisation.

Of course, this component of the barrier to imitation is only temporary. Sooner or later bankers will understand (as some of them have started to do) that in order to combat the erosion of their market share they have to adopt technological applications similar to those of their competitors. This means using data warehousing and mining, probably with a different form of market segmentation, based on actual purchasing behaviour rather than income groups or other methods of social categorisation. Within the retail market in general, we have seen this phenomenon in the increasingly widespread use of loyalty cards, which started as an innovation and have clearly become a commodity.

Intellectual inertia is useful for the first adopters of new technological applications, since it gives them a breathing space to get their houses in order. It is short-lived, however, and, like the element of surprise in military conflict, cannot be relied upon for any length of time.

How then do we ensure longer-lived sustainability? It is our view, supported by Venkatraman's early work, that technology alone, while able to confer some early advantage, cannot enable sustainability. While differentiation can come from technology, sustainability has to come from a different source – that source being the degree of change or transformation applied to the organisation in order to leverage the new application to the maximum. In this way, we can visualise a continuation of transformation linked to the adoption of a particular technology. We start with simple adoption, training people to use the new technology, and we progress to making significant changes in processes, mindsets, culture and behaviour, products and services, and organisational structure.

Clearly, the greater the degree of transformation of the organisation connected with technology, the greater the barrier to imitation and therefore the greater the sustainability of the new advantage. This is based on the principle that technology is visible, identifiable and buyable, while company culture, mindset and behaviour are hardly visible to the outside world, not readily identifiable and certainly not buyable! It is therefore the combination of technology and transformation that creates sustainable competitive advantage. Because this point is poorly understood by business leaders and technologists alike, technology has been relegated to a support role for business strategy while its ability to confer new advantage has been discounted or at best used only to gain first mover's advantage.

INDEX

3Com 49, 191
accessibility 38–41
acquisitions 14–16, 18
adapters 5–6, 35
AgrEvo 203
Air Miles 45
Air Products and Chemicals 83
Ali, Muhammad 42
aligning the organisation 66–7, 183
alliances *see* strategic allies
Amazon 167, 207
ANC (Aviate, Navigate, Communicate)
    principle 195–7
Andersen Consulting 133
Anglogold 69
Apple 37, 38, 49, 83, 88
AT&T 100–1, 108, 123, 133, 165
Autodesk 82
Avon Cosmetics 115

Banc One 26
banking 72–3, 105, 131, 148, 198, 208
    competition 21–2, 134–5
    cross-selling 57–8
    money traders 69–70
The Beatles 50–1
benchmarking 17
Berezovsky, Boris 163
Berkshire Hathaway 158
Betamax 39–40, 88
BP 123, 149
Branson, Richard 22, 26, 51, 52–3, 76, 103
Braund, Stephen 203

British Airways (BA) 44–5, 53, 68, 101
British Gas 173
British Satellite Broadcasting (BSB) 25
Brown-Humes, Christopher 148
Bruce Friesen, G. 89–90
Buffett, Warren 15, 158
bundling 58, 104–6, 149
business managers 76, 96, 116–17, 145–7,
    193, 194
Business Process Re-engineering (BPR)
    17
business-to-business relationships 135–7,
    138, 140–1, 149

Cable News Network (CNN) 47–8
Canon 134
capability 67, 184, 185–8
Capital One 81
capitalism 156–7, 158, 159–63
Carpoint 166
Carrier 123
Castrol 138
change 4, 13–14, 19–22, 75, 208–9
    discontinuities 11, 21
    seven levers of 7, 59, 62–4
Chrysler 15
civil service 67–8
Clinton, Hilary 163
Club Med 132–3
Coca-Cola 20, 136, 138
codified business practices (CBPs) 71, 73,
    74
Compaq 19, 83, 133, 141–2

competition 7–8, 17, 19–22, 38–41, 163
  Enterprise Systems 82–3
  information technology 201, 207–9
  for stakeholders 93–126
complacency 21, 29, 61, 86–7
computer technology 45–7, 48–50, 82–4,
  100
  see also high-technology companies
  customer relationships 136–8, 141–2
  ERPS 201, 202–7
  Microsoft/Apple conflict 36–7, 38–9
convenience 56, 105–6
Corzine, Robert 118
cross-selling 57–8
culture 59, 62, 63, 64, 78–81, 186–8
customer wheel 101, 102, 103, 104
customers 8–9, 85, 164–5, 184–5, 198
  competition 7–8, 95
  databases 17
  partnership 149–50
  relationships with 16, 22–3, 52–8, 130–
    42, 149
  staff relationship 67–8
  as stakeholders 97, 98, 100–7, 126
customisation 139–40, 165, 184–5, 186

Daimler-Benz 15
Davenport, Thomas 82
Dell Computer 19, 82, 137–8
demergers 16
departmentalisation 63, 72–3
Dijkgraaf, Henk 119
Direct Line 40, 135
direct-to-consumer relationship 134,
  135–8
discontinuities 4, 11, 21, 23–7, 33, 41, 65
Disney 43–4, 131–2, 140
Dolby 137
downsizing 17
Doyle, Chris 122

e-commerce 64, 123, 165, 202
Eastman Chemical Company 111–12
effectiveness 71
efficiency 71
Elf Atochem North America 83–4
employees 59, 62, 63, 64, 67–71, 183–92
  business manager distinction 117
  competition 95
  organisational structure 76, 77
  relationships with 145–7
  as shareholders 53, 70–1, 77
  as stakeholders 97, 98, 110–14
  symbols 80
wage claims 99–100
Encyclopaedia Britannica 46–7
Engel, Debra 191

Enterprise Resource Planning Systems
  (ERPS) 17, 201, 202–7
Enterprise Systems (ES) 82–4
environmental issues 118, 119
Ericsson 168–9
Ernst & Young 133
event-management 105–6
Expedia 166
extranets 84–5
Exxon 149

faddism 16–17
fashion design 86
Federal Express 19
financial control 78, 193–200
financial services 120–2, 135
fitness for purpose 65–7, 183, 185, 192
Forte 109–10
Fortune magazine 30, 117
Foxmeyer Drug 82
Fresh Horizons 171–80
frustration gap 67, 75, 86
Fuji 133
future forecasting 4–5, 28–9, 65, 168–70

Gates, Bill 26, 36–7, 38–9, 45–6, 80, 162
GE Capital 135
GE Medical Systems 76
General Dynamics 31
General Electric 9, 22, 101, 112–13, 114
General Motors 166
Gillette 137
Glaser, Rob 39
globalisation 46, 124, 151, 154–5, 160, 161
Godsell, Bobby 69
Goldsmith, James 15
Granada 109–10
Greenpeace 118, 119, 164

Hamel, Gary 15–16, 56–7
Hanson Group 14–15
Hanson, James 15
Hawkins, Jeff 49–50
Haynes, Brian 25
Hewlett-Packard 133
hierarchy 190–1
high-technology companies 19, 30, 36–41,
  48–50, 100–1, 167, 191
Honda 85–7, 90

IBM 24, 38–9, 81, 82, 85, 88–90, 133
ICI 16
identity 63
IKEA 132, 140
individualism 152, 156–7
information technology 151, 155, 165,
  167, 201–9

see also computer technology
innovation 16, 40, 47–51, 167–8
Intel 19, 136–7, 141
intellectual inertia 208
Internet 24, 48–9, 155, 202
  business through 41, 150, 165–6
  shopping 57
intranets 84
investment 87, 88–90
Iridium 148–9
ITT 76

Jennings, John 118
Jetform 133
Jobs, Steve 37
John Lewis Partnership 70–1
Johnson, Gerry 79
joint ventures 123–4
JVC 39–40

Kehoe, Louise 165–6
Kinepolis 54–5
King, Larry 48
King, Lord 44
knowledge 116–17, 155, 185–6
Kovacevich, Dick 57, 131
KPMG 80, 101, 147, 169

Larry King Live show 48
Law, Andy 77
Leeson, Nick 70
loyalty 97, 98–9, 106–7, 112, 113, 139
loyalty cards 134–5, 208

McKinsey consultancy 114
magnetic-strip cards 87–8
management *see* business managers
manufacturers 142–4, 204
market research 8–9
Market Value Builder (MVB) 113–14
markets 152, 154, 158–9
Marks & Spencer 9, 26–7, 108, 144, 207
Martin, Peter 141–2
MBNA 107
measurement, financial 78, 193–5, 196, 197–9
Medio Multimedia 30
mergers 14–16, 18
Microsoft 30, 45–6, 47, 48–9, 50, 133
  antitrust trial 162–3
  Apple comparison 36–7, 38–9
  discontinuities 24, 26, 41
  diversification 166–7
  employee-shareholders 70
  office design 80–1
  venture capital 19
Minitel 40–1

Mobil 122–3, 149
Mobil Europe 82
money traders 69–70, 111
monopolies 65, 141, 163
Moss Kanter, Rosabeth 76
motivation 67, 68–9, 184, 188–90
MSFDC 166–7
Murdoch, Rupert 24–6, 146, 162, 163
mutual gain 124–5, 144

National Health Service (NHS) 73, 79, 80
NatWest 45, 72, 148
Nestlé 116
Netscape 48–9
networking 140–1, 144, 150
New Zealand All Blacks 43
News Corporation 146, 162
Nicholson, Nigel 91–2
Nicolas wine merchant 54
Nishimuro, Taizo 123
Northern Foods 144
Norwest 57

object-orientated programming languages 206–7
Occidental Petroleum 30
office design 80–1
opportunity 67, 184, 190–1
Oracle 133, 202

Palm Pilot 49–50
Pascale, Richard 85–7, 90, 92
PAYU (Pay As You Use) system 115
pensions scandal 120–2
people 59, 62, 63, 64, 67–71, 183–92
  see also employees
Pepsi-Cola 20, 138
performance measurement 188–9
Peters and Waterman 16
privatisation 18, 44, 68, 157, 184
process 59, 62, 63, 64, 71–4
products and services 59, 62, 63, 64, 85–90, 149
Prudential Corporation 121
purchasing systems 204

quality control 71
Quinn Mills, D. 89–90

regulators 96, 97, 117–22, 126
Reichheld, F. F. 107
relationships 115, 116, 126–50
retail triangle 135–6
rewards 69–70, 111, 187, 189
risk 3, 50–1, 70, 91
Robinson, Gerry 109, 110
Rohwer, Jim 160–1

routine 79
Royal Bank of Scotland 148
rugby analogy 42–3
rule changing 5–6, 20–1, 41–2, 44, 65

St Lukes's advertising agency 77
Saro-Wiwa, Ken 118
Sculley, John 20
securitisation 158–9, 161
Seiko 137
Seinfeld, Jerry 90–1
services *see* products and services
seven levers of change 7, 59, 62–4
'shapers' 5, 6–7, 35
shareholders 95, 97, 107–10
　see also securitisation
　employees as 53, 70–1, 77
　takeovers 15
Shawcross, William 162
Shell 45, 117–19, 120, 149, 164
Silicon Graphics 30
Silicon Valley 19
Sky Television 24–5
small organisations 71–2, 77
smart cards 87–8, 171–2
solidarity 152, 159–60
Sony 39–40
Soros, George 158
staff *see* employees
Staino, Ed 149
stakeholders 8, 9, 93–126, 129, 130
Star TV 162
stories 79–80
strategic allies 96, 97, 122–5, 147–9
strategy 59, 62, 64–7, 183
structure 59, 62, 63, 64, 75–8, 190–2
Sun Microsystems 19
supermarkets 22, 134–5, 148, 164
suppliers 95, 97, 114–16, 142–5, 204
sustainable competitive advantage 201,
　207–9
switching costs 99, 113, 135, 191
symbols 80, 81

takeovers 14–16, 18

technology 59, 62, 63, 64, 81–5
　see also high-technology companies;
　　information technology
　discontinuities 24
　investment 88–90
　suppliers 116
telecommunications 40–1, 100–1, 148–9,
　168–9, 173
Tenneco 30
Tesco 148
Toshiba 123–4, 133
Total Quality Management (TQM) 17, 120
training 68, 71, 113, 186, 189

uncertainty 156
Unisys 31
Unocal 31
US Railways 78

value, shareholders 15, 108
value curve 35–6
value propositions 8, 9, 97–9
　business managers 117
　customers 100, 101, 107
　employees 110–11, 112
　strategic alliances 124
'Values Charter' 147
Venkatraman, N. 206, 208
venture capital 19, 167–8
victims 5, 6, 35, 63
Video Homes Systems (VHS) 39–40, 41
video technology 39–40
Virgin 9, 22, 26, 51–2, 76, 135, 207
Virgin Atlantic Airways 52–3, 101, 102–3
Visa 26

Wal-Mart 56–7, 207
Wang Laboratories 81
Welch, Jack 101, 112
Wells Fargo 57, 131
Wells, H.G. 13
'Work Out' consultation 112–13, 114
Wrigley's 137

Xerox 133, 134